✔ KT-177-142

WITHDRAWN

C016692267

Contents

Plan Your Trip

Jambalaya BRENT HOFACKER/SHUTTERSTOCK ©

Explore New Orleans 29

Survival Guide 147

Special Features

Contents

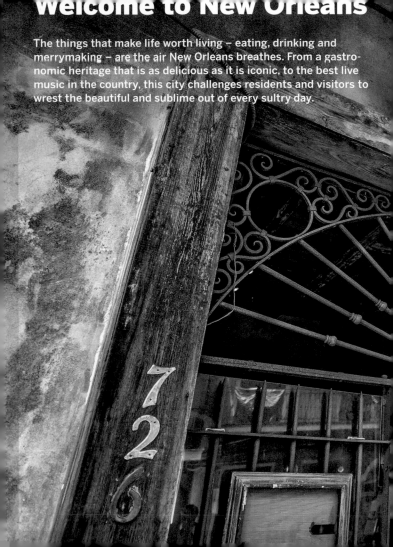

Welcome to New Orleans

The things that make life worth living – eating, drinking and merrymaking – are the air New Orleans breathes. From a gastronomic heritage that is as delicious as it is iconic, to the best live music in the country, this city challenges residents and visitors to wrest the beautiful and sublime out of every sultry day.

Preservation Hall (p52), French Quarter
F11PHOTO/SHUTTERSTOCK ©

Top Sights

TRAVELVIEW/SHUTTERSTOCK ©

Royal Street
Vibrant street in the French Quarter. **p32**

Jackson Square

Lively heart of the Quarter. **p36**

Lafayette Cemetery No 1

Tropical cemetery of your gothic dreams. **p90**

St Charles Avenue Streetcar

Romantic public transportation from days past. **p106**

KRIS DAVIDSON/LONELY PLANET ©

CSPFOTOIMAGES/GETTY IMAGES ©

LEGACY1995/SHUTTERSTOCK ©

Ogden Museum of Southern Art

A feast for the eyes. **p74**

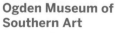

Cabildo

Historic museum on Jackson Square. **p34**

City Park

New Orleans' largest green space. **p122**

Audubon Zoo

Impressive zoo with awesome animals. **p108**

National WWII Museum

World War II from the US perspective. **p72**

Eating

In what other American city do people celebrate the harvest season of sewage-dwelling crustaceans? The crawfish boil (pictured right) exemplifies New Orleans' relationship with food: unconditional love. This city finds itself in its food; meals are both expressions of identity and bridges between the city's many divisions.

A Gastronomic Playground

We hope you're not reading this at home. We hope you're *in* New Orleans, because you're about to eat better than most others. When it comes to food, New Orleans does not fool around. Well, OK, it does: its playful attitude to ingredients and recipes mixes (for example) alligator sausage and cheesecake into a dessert fit for the gods. This sense of gastronomic play is rooted in both deep traditions – truly, this city has one of the few indigenous cuisines

in the country – and, increasingly, a willingness to accommodate outside influences, both in terms of technique and ethnicity.

Born on the Bayou

Settlers who arrived in Louisiana had to work with the ingredients of the bayous, woods and prairie, and so developed one of America's only true native-born cuisines. As a result, some say the New Orleans palette is limited to its own specialties, that this is a town of 'a thousand restaurants and three dishes.'

That cliché is a bit tired. First, lots of restaurants are serving what we would deem 'Nouveau New Orleans' cuisine – native classics influenced by global flavors and techniques. And, second, international options are popping up more frequently in this town.

Best For Foodies

Marjie's Grill Southeast Asian street food done with care and attention. (p128)

Bacchanal Wine, cheese, bread and a magically lit garden. (p62)

Seaworthy Incredibly fresh seafood, prepared with care and expertise. (p82)

Boucherie Southern cuisine cooked with fascinating new twists. (p114)

Classic Creole Cuisine

Commander's Palace This Garden District institution is the grande dame of classic Creole cuisine. (p97)

Gautreau's A lovely Uptown establishment that nails the New Orleans approach to food. (p114)

Restaurant August An elegant setting and presentation belies a gorgeous tableau of New Orleans dishes. (p83)

Herbsaint We'd fight people just for another taste of the gumbo. (p84)

'Nouveau New Orleans' Cuisine

Peche Seafood Grill One of the most highly regarded seafood restaurants in the USA. (p81)

SoBou Funky French Quarter restaurant that's decadent and playful with New Orleans recipes. (p45)

Bayona Local ingredients are buttressed by an international approach to cooking techniques. (p44)

Compère Lapin Creole Louisiana meets the gastronomy of the Caribbean. (p82)

Best for Po'boys

Parkway Tavern Grab a po'boy and enjoy a picnic on the banks of Bayou St John. (p129)

Rampart Food Store This convenience store has perfected the recipe for a shrimp sandwich. (p64)

Live Music

There is great live music happening every night of the week in New Orleans, which makes a strong claim to being the best live-music city in the nation. Jazz is definitely not the only genre on offer: R&B, rock, country, Cajun, zydeco, funk, soul, hip-hop and genre-defying experimentation are all common.

New Orleans Jazz & Heritage Festival

Jazz Fest sums up everything that would be lost if the world were to lose New Orleans. Much more than Mardi Gras, with its secret balls and sparkly trinkets, Jazz Fest reflects the generosity of New Orleans, its unstoppable urge to share its most precious resource – its culture – with the rest of the world. Of course, the Fest is first and foremost about music, but it isn't just about jazz. It's jazz *and* heritage, which means any music that jazz came from, and any music that jazz inspired. The multitude of stages and tents feature everything that pours in and out of jazz – blues, gospel, Afro-Caribbean, folk, country, zydeco, Cajun, funky brass, and on and on.

Bounce

Bounce is the defining sound of young black New Orleans. It's a high-speed genre distinct to the city that involves drum-machine-driven beats, call-and-response, sexualized lyrics and extremely raunchy dancing. Shows are led by DJs, who play a role similar to a selector at a Jamaican dancehall concert.

Best Live Music Overall

d.b.a. Live music pops off all the time, and the beer menu is extensive. (p68; pictured above)

Spotted Cat A fantastically dingy Frenchmen St dive for the quintessential New Orleans jazz show. (p67)

Tipitina's One of the city's most storied concert halls. (p118)

KOROZAA/SHUTTERSTOCK ©

Hi Ho Lounge An edgy little spot with a wide variety of music. (p67)

AllWays Lounge The place to go for an eclectic mix of genres and dance parties. (p67)

Best for Jazz

Spotted Cat A cozy dive bar that hosts some of the funkiest jazz acts in the city. (p67)

Snug Harbor Elegant bar with cocktail-attire-style service and classy acts. (p67)

Fritzel's European Jazz Pub Live jazz in a tiny venue where you're never more than ten feet from the performers. (p52)

Preservation Hall The guardian of the classic New Orleans jazz sound. (p52)

Chickie Wah Wah A locals' spot that features great music in the heart of Mid-City. (p132)

Best for Hip-Hop & Bounce

Blue Nile Hip-hop and dance hall acts regularly

take the stage at the Nile. (p69)

Siberia Bounce shows and serious booty-shaking are a regular occurrence. (p69)

Maison Younger hip-hop acts attract the college crowd at this Frenchmen St venue. (p69)

Tips for Gig-Goers

The standard cover charge for shows is $5 to $10. During events like Jazz Fest, however, seeing local celebrities like Kermit Ruffins may run to $15 or even $20.

Drinking & Nightlife

New Orleans doesn't rest for much. But the city isn't just a lush. A typical New Orleans night out features just as much food and music as booze. Here, all your senses are appealed to: your ear for a brass band, your taste for rich food, the touch of heat on your skin, and your whetted thirst for another shot.

Bars, Clubs & Lounges

In general, bars in New Orleans would often be considered 'dives' elsewhere. That's not to say bars here are grotty (although some certainly are); rather, there are many neighborhood joints in New Orleans that are unpretentious spots catering to those looking to drink, as opposed to those who want to meet and chat someone up. If you're in the latter category, head to lounges, which tend to be newer, more brightly lit and possessed of a general modern sensibility. That said, some bars, such as Mimi's in the Marigny, are good spots for both a beer after work and a bit of random flirtation.

Lowdown on the High Life

Most dedicated bars open around 5pm, although some places serve drinks during lunch, and some are open 24 hours. Closing time is an ill-defined thing; officially it's around 2am or 3am, but sometimes it's whenever the last customer stumbles out the door. It's common to leave a dollar or more for your bartender, even if they just pop the cap off a bottle of beer. You don't have to tip for every drink, but the general rule is to leave a couple of bucks extra for every hour spent at the bar.

Best Bars

Buffa's It's divey, the music is great, the drinks are strong, and it never closes. (p66)

Bar Tonique A bartenders' bar with great cocktails. (p49)

Tiki Tolteca Crazy mixed tropical drinks in a gloriously kitsch atmosphere. (p49)

GTS PRODUCTIONS/SHUTTERSTOCK ©

Mimi's in the Marigny
Mixed drinks, cold beer,
great music. (p65)

Twelve Mile Limit Casual
neighborhood vibe, great
spirits and drinks. (p130)

Cane & Table Expert mixed
drinks and a courtyard
plucked from tropical
fantasies. (p50)

Best Coffee

Fair Grinds Great coffee,
tasty baked goods, friendly
staff and an artsy cafe
atmosphere. (p132)

Station Strong coffee and
handmade pastries in Mid-
City. (p132)

Spitfire Coffee French
Quarter cafe dishing out
potent drip coffee a step
below rocket fuel. (p51)

Solo Espresso Artsy little
Bywater cafe that sources
coffee from around the
world. (p67)

Best Cocktails

Cane & Table Tropical
drinks mixed with a ton of
attention and skill. (p50)

French 75 A bar so
dedicated to cocktails it was
named for one. (p49)

Cure The bar that gentrified
Freret St on the strength of
its cocktail menu. (p117)

Treo The mixed drinks are
as creative as the artwork in
the on-site gallery. (p131)

Architecture

JOHN ELK/GETTY IMAGES ©

Beautiful New Orleans' architectural origins are French, Spanish, and 19th century American. All of these cultures began building here at a time when design tastes trended towards the romantic. The city's streetscape has long enamored artists – there's a reason so many local buildings are on the National Register of Historic Places.

Cross-section of a City

While there's more to the city's architecture than the French Quarter and Garden District, those neighborhoods do nicely illustrate the pronounced difference between the two 'sectors' of New Orleans: Creole and American. It's worth noting that there is no perfect split between the two sides of the city; Creole cottages can be found Uptown, and shotgun houses pack Bywater and the Marigny.

DIY Architectural Tour

A buck twenty-five gets you on the St Charles Avenue Streetcar, which plies the world's oldest continuously operating street railway system. It travels through the CBD, the Garden District and into Uptown/Riverbend, passing some of the city's prettiest buildings on the way.

Best Beautiful Buildings

New Orleans Museum of Art A classical-temple-styled icon of the city's arts scene. (p126)

Cabildo This Spanish-colonial classic now houses a Louisiana history museum. (p34; pictured above)

St Louis Cathedral A towering monument to the city's deep Catholic roots. (p42)

Royal Street Packed with gorgeous Caribbean-colonial townhouses and courtyards. (p32)

Shopping

JAMSEDEL/SHUTTERSTOCK ©

Too many travelers assume shopping in New Orleans equals unspeakable T-shirts from the French Quarter. Wrong! This is a creative town that attracts innovative entrepreneurs and features lovely vintage and antique stores, cutting-edge boutiques, functional art and amusing kitsch – and generally lacks the worst chain-store blah.

Best Shopping Overall

Kitchen Witch It's a book store – dedicated to cook books! Brilliant. (p145)

Fifi Mahony's Wild wigs and costuming craziness. (p53)

Tchoup Industries Handmade bags and accessories created from local materials. (p102)

SecondLine Art & Antiques Great chance to meet and mingle with the artists and support local talent. (p54)

Disko Obscura Funky niche shop specializing in underground synth. (p102)

Best Souvenirs

Palace Market A boutique art market for those seeking a unique gift from New Orleans. (p61)

Home Malone Filled to the brim with New Orleans–inspired gifts and goodness. (p133)

I.J. Reilly's Awesome gifts and objets d'art with an identifiable New Orleans twist. (p68)

Festivals

SIOUXSNAPP/SHUTTERSTOCK ©

Between late January, when Carnival Season begins, and late April/early May, when Jazz Fest happens, it's pretty much back-to-back celebrations in New Orleans. There are lulls here and there, but by the time mid-March rolls around it feels like there's a small festival bridging these two big events every weekend.

The Big Two

No two events encapsulate New Orleans like Mardi Gras and Jazz Fest. These festivals are more than celebrations: they contain within themselves every thread of the colorful, complicated New Orleans tapestry.

Best Festivals

Mardi Gras (www.mardigrasneworleans.com) In February or early March, Fat Tuesday marks the orgasmic finale of the Carnival season. Expect parades, floats, insane costumes, and a day of absolute madcap revelry as the entire city throws down for an all-day party.

Jazz Fest (www.nojazzfest. com; entrances at Fortin St, Far Grounds Race Course; adult/child $80/5; ☺last weekend in Apr & first weekend in May) Held during the last weekend of April and the first weekend of May, this extravaganza of music, food, crafts and good living is a mainstay of the New Orleans festival calendar, attracting both international headliners and local artists. Tickets are cheaper if you order in advance.

St Joseph's Day – Super Sunday (2600 Lasalle St, AL Davis Park; ☺Mar) March 19 and its nearest Sunday bring 'gangs' of Mardi Gras Indians out onto the streets in all their drumming glory. The Super Sunday parade usually begins around noon at AL Davis Park in Central City.

Mid-City Bayou Boogaloo (Bayou Boogaloo; www. thebayouboogaloo.com; Bayou St John, Moss St & Orleans Ave; admission free; ☺mid-May; ♦♟) Bayou Boogaloo is a great 'shoulder season' festival that features live music, (usually) pleasant weather and a general sense of conviviality. Folks gather on the green space that runs along Bayou St John.

San Fermin in Nueva Orleans (http://nolabulls. com; ☺mid-July) New Orleanians recreate Spain's running of the bulls...sort of. Thousands dress in white and wear red scarves, proceed to get rip roaring drunk, and then run through the streets chased by 'bulls'...roller derby girls with horned helmets brandishing plastic baseball bats.

Tours

ZACK FRANK/SHUTTERSTOCK ©

Sometimes it feels as if there are more guided tours of this city than actual residents. Tours allow visitors to digest the enormity of New Orleans with a knowledgeable mentor – get the right tour guide, and entirely new levels of the city will be revealed that you could never have accessed on your own.

Ghostly Encounters

The most popular tours in town are ghost tours, which tend to be a little cheesy and oddly sanitized. The ghost tour guides make a big deal about how they'll show you the macabre side of the city, but they seem to always discuss one-off murders, not, for example, the city's brutal, bloody history of slavery.

Stroll or Roll

Serious walking tours can be found via local nonprofits and educational institutions. You might also consider taking a bicycle tour – New Orleans is flat, and while the potholes could devour a horse, it is easy to pedal around.

Best Tours

Confederacy of Cruisers (📞504 400 5468; www.confederacyof-cruisers.com; 634 Elysian Fields Ave; tours $49-89) Get on two wheels and take in architecture, restaurants and bars.

Friends of the Cabildo (📞504-523-3939; www.friendsofthecabildo.org; 523 St Ann St; adult/student $20/15; ⏰10am & 1:30pm Mon-Sun) A walking tour that takes in the nuances of the city's deep history.

Kayakitiyat (📞985-778-5034, 512-964-9499; http://kayakitiyat.com; tours per person $45-105) Get out on a boat and explore the waterways that thread through the city.

Save Our Cemeteries (📞504-525-3377; www.saveourcemeteries.org; adult/child under 12yr $15/free; ⏰tours 10:30am & 1pm) Thoughtful tours of the 'cities of the dead' that pepper the landscape.

Tours By Judy (📞504-416-7777, 504-416-6666; www.toursbyjudy.com; per person from $15) Explore the city with tours crafted by a dedicated local historian.

For Kids

MICHA WEBER/SHUTTERSTOCK ©

New Orleans is a fairy-tale city, with its weekly costume parties and daily music wafting through the air. The same flights of fancy and whimsy that give this city such appeal for poets and artists also make it an imaginative wonderland for children, especially creative ones.

Festival Fun

The many street parties and outdoor festivals of New Orleans bring food stalls and, of course, great music. Children will love dancing to the beat. Seek out festivals held during the day, such as Bayou Boogaloo (www.thebayouboogaloo.com).

Best Kid-Friendly Spots for Exploring the City

Louisiana Children's Museum A good introduction to the region for toddlers. (p80)

Cabildo A history museum that older kids will appreciate. (p34)

Presbytère Dive into the pomp and pageantry of Mardi Gras. (p43)

Latter Library A good selection of children's literature in a pretty historical mansion. (p114)

Lafayette Cemetery No 1 City cemeteries are authentic slices of the past and enjoyably spooky to boot. (p90)

Top Tips for Travel with Children

From April until October it can be oppressively hot and humid. Bring cool, airy clothes and, whenever you head outside, take liquid for hydration. New Orleans' sidewalks are often horrible for strollers – you'll want to bring one that is both maneuverable and durable. Most restaurants have high chairs and booster seats and are happy to accommodate kids. Call ahead to make sure.

LGBT New Orleans

MICHA WEBER/SHUTTERSTOCK ©

Louisiana is a culturally conservative state, but its largest city bucks that trend. New Orleans is one of the oldest gay-friendly cities in the Western hemisphere, marketing itself as the 'Gay Capital of the South.' Neighborhoods such as the French Quarter and Marigny are major destinations on the LGBT travel circuit.

The Vibe

New Orleans is a pretty integrated city. Except for the lower part of Bourbon St, few areas or businesses feel exclusively gay. Rather, the queer vibe in the city seems to be strongest during major festivals such as the Gay Easter Parade and Southern Decadence.

Southern Safe Haven

New Orleans has always had a reputation as a city for outcasts, which for much of history has included the gay and lesbian population. Even today, in conservative states such as Alabama and Mississippi, gay and lesbian youth feel the pull of the Big Easy, where acceptance of their sexuality isn't hard to find.

Best Gay & Lesbian Bars

Country Club Good drinks and food, and a pool in a tropical courtyard. (p66)

Bourbon Pub & Parade A big, over-the-top gay bar that anchors the Quarter's LGBT scene. (p52)

AllWays Lounge Frequently puts on cabaret and drag shows. (p67)

Four Perfect Days

Day 1

JORG HACKEMANN/SHUTTERSTOCK ©

Wake up and smell the coffee in the French Quarter at **Croissant D'Or Patisserie** (p46). Afterwards, take a stroll around the streets as they wake up, and then sign up for the **Friends of the Cabildo** (p19) walking tour. Have lunch at **Mister Gregory's** (p46), then wander through **Jackson Square** (p36), the green heart of the neighborhood. Later, explore the Quarter's museums, such as the **Cabildo** (p34) and **Presbytère** (p43). Afterwards, enjoy a free afternoon concert at the **Old US Mint** (p42). Have dinner at **Bayona** (p44), then relax with a drink at **Bar Tonique** (p49) or **French 75** (p49), two of the finest cocktail bars in the city. Afterward, take in a show at **Preservation Hall** (p52) or **One Eyed Jacks** (p53).

Day 2

JIAWANGKUN/SHUTTERSTOCK ©

Head to the CBD & Warehouse District and spend a morning at the **Ogden Museum of Southern Art** (p74). Have lunch at **Cochon Butcher** (p84) for artisan meats with a Cajun twist. Now head to the Garden District and stroll along pretty Magazine St. Walk north, pop into **Lafayette Cemetery No 1** (p90) and hop on the **St Charles Avenue Streetcar** (p106; pictured above), heading west toward Uptown. Along the way, you'll soak up the lovely architecture and appreciate the shade of the live oak trees along St Charles Ave. Afterwards, continue along the streetcar towards the Riverbend. Enjoy creative Vietnamese cuisine at **Ba Chi Canteen** (p115) for dinner, then finish the night rocking out at **Maple Leaf Bar** (p118) or **Tipitina's** (p118).

Day 3

We're heading to Faubourg Marigny and having a crab omelette at **Cake Café & Bakery** (p62). Join the morning Creole Neighborhoods cycle tour with **Confederacy of Cruisers** (p19), or just lose yourself amidst all of the candy colored houses in the Marigny. Lunch? The **Lost Love** (p64) bar has a surprise Vietnamese kitchen. Walk east along Royal or Congress Sts and check out the riot of rainbow residences. Once you pass Press St, you're in Bywater. Take a walk into **Crescent Park** (p61; pictured above), where you can enjoy great views of the Mississippi. For dinner, have wine and cheese in a musical garden at **Bacchanal** (p62), then head back into Faubourg Marigny for live music on St Claude Ave or Frenchmen St.

Day 4

Rent a bicycle and ride around the Tremé; Governor Nicholls St is particularly pretty. Don't miss the **Backstreet Cultural Museum** (p138). From here, it's an easy walk into **Louis Armstrong Park** (p138). For lunch, get the fried chicken at **Willie Mae's Scotch House** (p141). Then head up **Esplanade Avenue** (p126) and gawk at the Creole mansions (pictured above). Take Esplanade all the way to **City Park** (p122) and wander around the **New Orleans Museum of Art** (p126). Afterwards, relax along the banks of bucolic **Bayou St John** (p126). For dinner, **Café Degas** (p129) has a romantic French atmosphere. Have a drink at friendly **Pal's** (p131), and consider catching more live music at a favorite venue you've discovered on your trip.

Need to Know
For detailed information, see Survival Guide (p147)

Currency
US dollars ($)

Money
ATMs are widely available.

Language
English, Spanish

Time
Central Time (GMT/ UTC minus six hours)

Tipping
Mandatory. At restaurants, tip 18% for good service, 20% for exceptional service.

Visas
Visas are required for most foreign visitors unless eligible for the Visa Waiver Program (VWP). Note that nationals of waiver countries who have traveled to Iran, Iraq, Libya, Somalia, Sudan, Syria, or Yemen after March 1, 2011 are no longer eligible for the VWP. In addition, nationals of VWP countries who are also nationals of these seven nations no longer qualify for a waiver.

Daily Budget

Budget: Less than $150
Dorm bed: $30

Self-cater or cheap takeout meal: $10

Beer at local bar: $3–5

Bicycle rental: $20

All-day streetcar pass: $3

Midrange: $150–250
Guesthouse or B&B double room: $100–150

Neighborhood restaurant meal for two: $50–70

Bicycle rental or split taxi fares: $20–40

Top end: More than $250
Fine dining for two, plus wine: $150–200

Four-star double hotel rooms: from $200

Taxis or car rental: $40–60

Advance Planning

Three months before Check if any festivals are going down; book hotel rooms if you're arriving during Mardi Gras or Jazz Fest.

One month before Organize car rental. Make bookings at high-end restaurants you don't want to miss.

One week before Read *Gambit* (www. bestofneworleans.com) and check www. neworleansonline.com to see what's going on in the way of live music during your visit.

Arriving in New Orleans

The majority of travelers to New Orleans will arrive by air via Louis Armstrong New Orleans International Airport (MSY). Greyhound (www.greyhound.com) buses and Amtrak trains stop at Union Passenger Terminal, also known as Union Station.

✈ Louis Armstrong New Orleans International Airport

13 miles west of the city along I-10.

Shuttle 24 hours, one-way/round trip $24/44

Bus E2 Airport Downtown Express every 70 minutes 5am-10pm Mon-Fri, 6:30am-10:20pm Sat & Sun

Taxi 24 hours, flat rate $36 for one or two passengers, $15 per person for three or more passengers

🚆🚆 Union Passenger Terminal

Bus Linked to several bus lines, $1.25 fare

Taxi $8-10 French Quarter

Getting Around

The New Orleans Regional Transit Authority (www.norta.com) sells 1/3/5 day Jazzy Passes ($3/9/15) that you can download onto your smartphone, for use on buses and streetcars.

🚋 Streetcars

New Orleans' streetcars are charming, but the service only covers a relatively small part of the city. One-way fares cost $1.25, and multitrip passes are available.

🚶 Walk

If you're just exploring the French Quarter, your feet will serve you just fine.

🚲 Cycle

Flat New Orleans is easy to cycle – you can cross the entirety of town in 45 minutes. Blue Bikes (📞504-608-0603; http://nola.socialbicycles.com; per hr $8) bike-share kiosks are located around town.

New Orleans Neighborhoods

Mid-City, Bayou St John & City Park (p121)
This gorgeous residential area abuts the lovely City Park and offers both lush greenery and urban character.

◉ *City Park*

Uptown & Riverbend (p105)
Student scene, mansions, high-end shopping and haute cuisine combine in one of New Orleans' most beautiful neighborhoods.

St Charles Avenue Streetcar ◉

Lafayette Cemetery No 1 ◉

◉ *Audubon Zoo*

Garden, Lower Garden & Central City (p89)
Enormous live oak trees shade an affluent neighborhood intersected by parade routes, countless cafes and student bars.

Tremé-Lafitte (p135)
The oldest African American neighborhood in the country has its finger firmly on the cultural pulse of the city.

Faubourg Marigny & Bywater (p57)
These two bohemian neighborhoods represent the artsy, gentrified edge of the city. Innovative bars, food and unbeatable live music abound.

Cabildo
Royal Street
Jackson Square

Ogden Museum of Southern Art
National WWII Museum

French Quarter (p31)
A tight concentration of historical buildings that contains an adult theme park centered on food, drink and music.

CBD & Warehouse District (p71)
The traditional downtown business district, peppered with red-brick, reconstituted warehouses and high-rises.

Explore
New Orleans

New Orleans' Walking Tours 🚶

St Charles Avenue Streetcar (p106) TRAVELVIEW/SHUTTERSTOCK ©

Explore

French Quarter

Also known as Vieux Carré ('voo car-ray': Old Quarter) and 'the Quarter', the French Quarter is the original city as planned by the French in the 1800s. Here lies the infamous Bourbon St, but of more interest is an elegantly aged grid of shopfronts and courtyard gardens. The Quarter is great, but, admittedly, it's kind of a theme park: heavy on tourist traffic and light on locals (apart from your bartender or waiter).

Start exploring with a walking tour and consider catching a concert sponsored by the National Park Service at the New Orleans Jazz Museum (p42). Finish the evening with dinner at either Coop's Place (p45) or Galatoire's (p45), and drinks at Cane & Table (p50). On the next day, walk up and down Royal St (p32) and get yourself to Preservation Hall (p52) early enough to see the show.

Getting There & Around

The Quarter is well connected by public transportation to the rest of the city. The entire neighborhood is easily walkable. Parking is a hassle.

🚊 The Canal, Rampart and Riverfront streetcars all skirt the edges of the French Quarter.

🚌 Bus 91 runs up Rampart St and Esplanade Ave, which both border the French Quarter.

Neighborhood Map on p40

Top Sight 📷
Royal Street

Royal St, with its antiques shops, galleries, and potted ferns hanging from cast-iron balconies, is the elegant yin to well-known Bourbon St's debauched yang. Stroll or bicycle past Royal's patina of beauty and fading grace; chat with locals as they lounge on their porches; and get a sense of the fun – with a dash of elegance – that was once the soul of the Vieux Carré.

◉ MAP P40, A8

Outdoor Arcade

Royal St is one of the places where soul still exists in New Orleans. Blocks and blocks of the strip are dedicated to antiques stores and art galleries, making Royal a sort of elegant 19th-century (and very long) outdoor shopping arcade. But there's no getting around the fact that far more visitors have heard of, and spend time on, Bourbon St than Royal St. And to be fair, Royal St is, in a sense, as artificial and manufactured as Bourbon St.

Balconies & Courtyards

Few people actually live on the 13 blocks that constitute the French Quarter stretch of Royal St, although they once did, as attested by rows of wrought-iron balconies and closely packed Creole town houses. You may not be able to tell from the street, but behind many of these buildings lie enormous gardens and leafy courtyards, once spaces of escape from the street scene, now often utilized as dining spaces by restaurants.

Pedestrian Performances

The blocks of Royal St between St Ann St and St Louis St are closed to vehicle traffic during the afternoon. Musicians, performers and other buskers set up shop; you may see some teenagers shill for pennies, or accomplished blues musicians jam on their Fenders. Either way, the show is almost always entertaining.

★ Top Tips

o Photographers should come early for great light and (nearly) empty streets.

o Buskers are at their best at brunch time on weekends.

o From 11am to 4pm, most of the street turns into a pedestrian-only mall.

o A guided walking tour will open your eyes to a lot of the hidden history here.

✗ Take a Break

Start off your Royal St adventure with coffee and pastries at Croissant D'Or Patisserie (p46).

Stop off for a tipple at the lovely, rotating Carousel Bar (p50) at the street's upper end.

Top Sight 📷
Cabildo

The former seat of power in colonial Louisiana serves as the gateway for exploring the history of the state, and New Orleans in particular. The Cabildo, a Spanish term for a city council, draws visitors into airy halls reminiscent of Spanish Colonial design, and features a mansard roof (the narrow, steep-sided roofs commonly found in Europe) added in French style.

👁 MAP P40, C5

📞 504-568-6985

http://louisianastatemuseum.org

701 Chartres St

adult/student/child under 6yr $6/5/free

🕐 10am-4:30pm Tue-Sun

Excellent Exhibits

The exhibits, from Native American tools on the 1st floor to 'Wanted' posters for escaped slaves on the 3rd, do a good job of reaffirming the role the building and the surrounding region have played in history. Highlights include an entire section dedicated to the Battle of New Orleans and a historical *Plan de la Nouvelle Orléans* from 1744, showing a four-block-deep city. Give yourself at least two hours to explore.

Sala Capitular

The magnificent Sala Capitular (Capitol Room), was the most important room in Louisiana for decades. Civic functions and legal action were conducted here; this was the courtroom where *Plessy v Ferguson*, the 1896 case that legalized segregation under the 'separate but equal' doctrine, was tried.

Reconstruction

American author William Faulkner wrote, 'The past is never dead. It's not even past.' That quote only begins to hint at the troubled history of race relations in the South. The wing of the Cabildo dedicated to post–Civil War Reconstruction is as even-handed and thorough an attempt at explaining this difficult period and its consequences as we've seen.

Cabildo History

Fire has played an important role in this building's story, both in its 1795 construction (after the Great New Orleans Fire of 1788, which tore through much of the Quarter, cleared this site of its existing structure) and two centuries later, when the Cabildo was burned in 1988. Painstakingly restored, and returned to its original glory, the building is a treasure in its own right – not to mention the treasures that are on display inside its halls.

★ Top Tips

○ Although the Cabildo is closed on Mondays, Friends of the Cabildo still offers walking tours, which are excellent.

○ Be sure to take a peek at Jackson Square out of the large windows on the 2nd floor.

○ Check http://louisianastatemuseum.org/events for current listings of events including concerts yoga and more.

✗ Take a Break

Make a day of it and have brunch at Court of the Two Sisters (p47), a few blocks away on Royal St.

A little further on, grab a well-earned drink at **Toulouse Dive Bar** (☏ 504-522-2260; 738 Toulouse St; ⏰2pm–6am Mon-Thu, 11am-7am Fri-Sun) and shoot a game of pool.

Top Sight
Jackson Square

*Whatever happens in the Quarter usually begins
here. Sprinkled with lazing loungers; surrounded
by fortune tellers, sketch artists and traveling
performers; and overlooked by cathedrals, offices
and shops, Jackson Square is one of America's
great town squares. It both anchors the French
Quarter and is the beating heart of this corner
of town. The street performers tend to do their
schtick in the early evening, just as the sun is
going down.*

◎ MAP P40, D5

Decatur & St Peter Sts

The Square's Root

The square was part of Adrien de Pauger's original city plan and began life as a military parade ground called Place d'Armes (Place of Weapons). Madame Micaëla Pontalba, a 19th-century aristocrat, transformed the muddy marching grounds into a trimmed garden and renamed the square to honor Andrew Jackson, the president who saved New Orleans from the British during the War of 1812. Today, along the edges of that garden you'll see street performers, artists, bands and tourists taking in the atmosphere. It's a gentle, carnivalesque scene, invariably lovely at sunset, which belies a bloody history: during the 1811 German Coast Slave Uprising, three leaders of the rebellion were hung here.

Centering the Square

Jackson Square is adjacent to some of New Orleans' most iconic buildings and institutions. The identical, block-long **Pontalba Buildings** overlook the scene, and the nearly identical **Cabildo** and **Presbytère** flank the impressive **St Louis Cathedral**, which fronts the square.

Jackson Monument

In the middle of the park stands the monument to Andrew Jackson (pictured left) – Clark Mills' bronze equestrian statue of the seventh US president, unveiled in 1856. The inscription, 'The Union Must and Shall be Preserved,' was added by General Benjamin Butler, Union military governor of New Orleans during the Civil War, ostensibly to rub it into the occupied city's face. The gesture worked. Butler was dubbed 'Beast Butler' by locals, and eventually his face was stamped on the bottom of city chamber pots. Butler deserves some credit too, however: during his tenure as military governor of New Orleans, he instituted health quarantines that drastically reduced yellow-fever outbreaks.

★ Top Tips

o Definitely tip something, even if it's just pocket change, for a good performance. That's why people perform here.

o Tarot card readers and fortune tellers stay well into the evening; some are open to bargaining when the foot traffic thins.

o Come on weekends just after brunch for 'prime time.'

✗ Take a Break

Hop into Stanley (p47), at the square's north corner; it's an iconic spot for brunch, lunch or drinks.

Across Decatur St from the square lies Café du Monde (p48), where you can grab a bag of beignets (square, sugar-coated fritters) to go and picnic on a park bench. Pigeon camaraderie is free.

Walking Tour 🥾

A Stroll in the Vieux Carré

Too many visitors to the French Quarter presume the only way around it is a stagger fueled by a neon-colored drink. Not so! On this tour, you'll get to soak up some of the finest architecture in this preserved neighborhood, with nary a bar on the itinerary (if that's not your thing, please proceed directly to the Drinking & Nightlife section, and have one for us).

Walk Facts

Start Jackson Sq
End Jackson Sq
Length 1.1 miles; 1½ hours

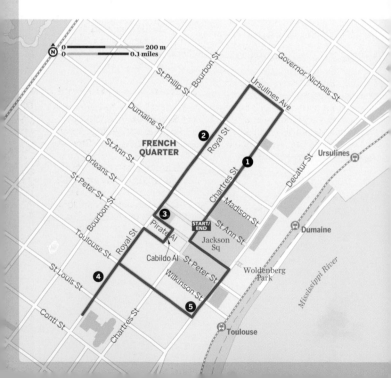

❶ Jackson Square to Ursulines Ave

Begin your walk at the Presbytère (p43) on Jackson Sq and head down Chartres St to the corner of Ursulines Ave. Directly across Chartres St, the Beauregard-Keyes House (p43) combines Creole and American styles of design. Walk along Ursulines Ave to Royal St – the soda fountain at the Royal Pharmacy is a preserved relic from halcyon malt-shop days.

❷ Along Royal Street

When it comes to quintessential New Orleans postcard images, Royal St takes the prize. Cast-iron galleries grace the buildings and a profusion of flowers garland the facades, while boisterous buskers blare their tunes from practically every street corner, often to wild acclaim. At No 915 Royal, the **Cornstalk Hotel** stands behind one of the most frequently photographed fences anywhere.

❸ Pirate's Alley

St Anthony's Garden (tough to see beyond the rows of street art)

sits behind St Louis Cathedral (p42). Alongside the garden, take Pirate's Alley and turn right down Cabildo Alley and then right up St Peter St toward Royal St. Tennessee Williams lived at No 632 St Peter in 1946–47 while he wrote *A Streetcar Named Desire*.

❹ Around the Historic New Orleans Collection

Turn left on Royal St. At the corner of Royal and Toulouse Sts stands a pair of houses built by Jean François Merieult in the 1790s. The building known as the Court of Two Lions, at 541 Royal St, opens onto Toulouse St and next door is the Historic New Orleans Collection (p42) museum.

❺ Return to Jackson Square

On the next block, the massive 1909 **State Supreme Court Building** was the setting for many scenes in director Oliver Stone's movie *JFK*.

Turn around and head right on Toulouse St to Decatur St and turn left. Cut across the road and walk the last stretch of this tour along the river back to Jackson Square.

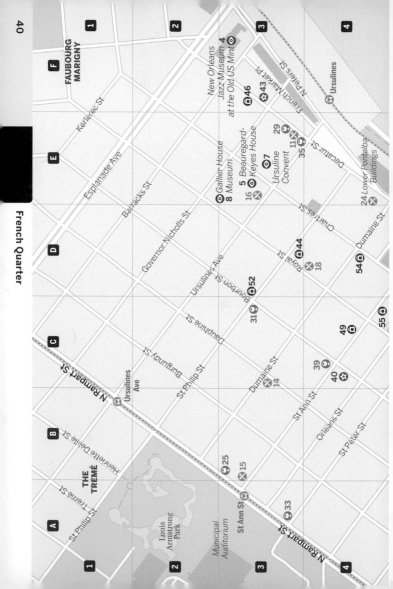

French Quarter

FAUBOURG
MARIGNY

THE TREMÉ

Louis Armstrong Park

Municipal Auditorium

New Orleans Jazz Museum 4 at the Old US Mint ◉

🔳46

⭐43

Gallier House 8 Museum, ◉

5 Beauregard-Keyes House ◉

16 ◉ ❌

Ursuline Convent ◉7

29 ◉ 🔳
11 ◉
35 ◉

24 Lower Pontalba Buildings

❌

44 ◉

18 ❌

54 🔳

52 🔳

31 ◉

49 🔳

55 🔳

39 ◉

40 ⭐

14 ◉

25 ◉

15 ❌

33 ◉

Kerlerec St

Esplanade Ave

Barracks St

Governor Nicholls St

Ursulines Ave

Bourbon St

Dauphine St

Burgundy St

St Philip St

Ursulines Ave

Henriette Delille St

Tremé St

St Philip St

St Ann St

Dumaine St

St Ann St

Orleans St

St Peter St

N Rampart St

N Rampart St

Decatur St

Chartres St

Royal St

Dumaine St

N Peters St

French Market Pl

Ursulines

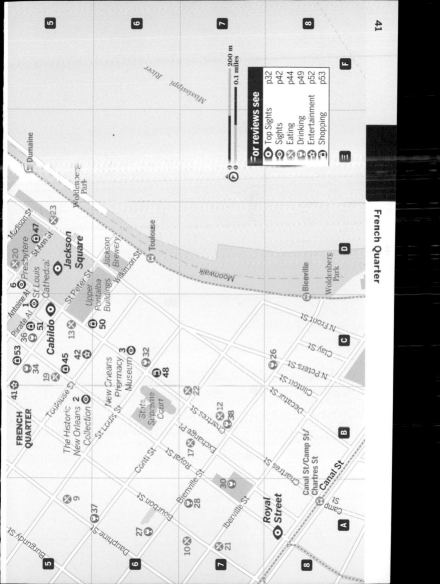

French Quarter

FRENCH QUARTER

Royal Street

Jackson Square

Cabildo

The Historic New Orleans Collection

New Orleans Pharmacy Museum

State Supreme Court

Presbytere

St Louis Cathedral

Upper Pontalba Buildings

Jackson Brewery

Moonwalk

Woldenberg Park

Mississippi River

For reviews see

⊙	Top Sights	p32
⊙	Sights	p42
⊗	Eating	p44
⊗⊗	Drinking	p49
⊕⊕	Entertainment	p52
⊕	Shopping	p53

200 m
0.1 miles

Antoine Al
Pirate Al
Madison St
St Ann St
St Peter St
St Louis St
Toulouse St
Conti St
Bienville St
Iberville St
Canal St/Camp St
Bourbon St
Royal St
Exchange Pl
Chartres St
Decatur St
N Peters St
N Front St
Clinton St
Clay St
Chartres St
Dauphine St
Burgundy St
Dumaine
Toulouse
Bienville
Woldenberg Park
Camp St
Canal St

FRENCH QUARTER

Sights

St Louis Cathedral CATHEDRAL

1 ◉ MAP P40, C5

One of the best examples of French architecture in the country, this triple-spired 18th-century cathedral is dedicated to Louis IX, the French king sainted in 1297. It's an attractive bit of Gallic heritage in the heart of an American city. In addition to hosting black, white and Creole Catholic congregants, St Louis has also attracted those who, in the best New Orleanian tradition, mix their influences, such as voodoo queen Marie Laveau. (☏504-525-9585; www.stlouisca-thedral.org; Jackson Sq; donations accepted, audio guide $8; ◷8am-4pm, Mass 12:05pm Mon-Fri, 5pm Sat, 9am & 11am Sun)

The Historic New Orleans Collection MUSEUM

2 ◉ MAP P40, B5

A combination of preserved buildings, museums and research centers all rolled into one, The Historic New Orleans Collection is a good introduction to the history of the city. The complex is anchored by its Royal St campus, which presents a series of regularly rotating exhibits and occasional temporary exhibits. Some of the artifacts on display include an original Jazz Fest poster, transfer documents of the Louisiana Purchase, and utterly disturbing slave advertisements.

(THNOC; ☏504-523-4662; www.hnoc.org; 533 Royal St; admission free, tours $5; ◷9:30am-4:30pm Tue-Sat, from 10:30am Sun, tours 10am, 11am, 2pm & 3pm Tue-Sat)

New Orleans Pharmacy Museum MUSEUM

3 ◉ MAP P40, C6

This beautifully preserved shop, groaning with ancient display cases filled with intriguing little bottles, was established in 1823 by Louis J Dufilho, at a time when the pharmaceutical arts were – shall we say – in their infancy. The museum suggests Dufilho was the nation's first licensed pharmacist, although today his practices would be suspect (gold-coated pills for the wealthy; opium, alcohol and cannabis for those with less cash). (☏504-565-8027; www.pharmacy-museum.org; 514 Chartres St; adult/student/child under 10yr $5/4/free; ◷10am-4pm Tue-Sat)

New Orleans Jazz Museum at the Old US Mint MUSEUM

4 ◉ MAP P40, F3

The Mint, a blocky Greek Revival structure, is the only building of its kind to have printed both US and Confederate currency. Today it is home to the New Orleans Jazz Museum, with rotating exhibits on local jazz history and culture. It also contains the Louisiana Historical Center, an archive of

JORG HACKEMANN/SHUTTERSTOCK ©

St Louis Cathedral

manuscripts, microfiche and records related to the state. **New Orleans Jazz National Historic Park** (☎504-589-4841; www.nps.gov/jazz; 916 N Peters St; admission free; ☺9am-4:30pm Tue-Thu, to 4pm Fri & Sat) hosts concerts here on weekday afternoons; check in at its office to see who is playing or visit the museum's website. (☎504 568-6993; www.nolajazzmuseum.org; 400 Esplanade Ave; adult/child $6/5; ☺10am-4:30pm Tue-Sun)

Beauregard-Keyes House
HISTORIC BUILDING

5 ◉ MAP P40, E3

This 1826 Greek Revival house is named for its two most famous former inhabitants. Confederate General Pierre Gustave Toutant

Beauregard commanded the artillery battery that fired the first shots at Fort Sumter in Charleston, SC, starting the Civil War. Frances Parkinson Keyes wrote 51 novels, many set in New Orleans (and many that had, let's say, not the most sympathetic depictions of African Americans, Jews, Italians and the Irish). Her collection of some 200 dolls and folk costumes are on display. (☎504 523-7257; www.bkhouse.org; 1113 Chartres St; tours adult/student/child $10/4/9; ☺tours hourly 10am-3pm Mon-Sat)

Presbytère
MUSEUM

6 ◉ MAP P40, D5

The lovely Presbytère building, designed in 1791 as a rectory for the St Louis Cathedral, serves as

New Orleans' Mardi Gras museum. You'll find there's more to the city's most famous celebration than wanton debauchery – or, at least, discover the many levels of meaning behind the debauchery. There's an encyclopedia's worth of material on the krewes (parade marching clubs), secret societies, costumes and racial histories that comprise the complex Mardi Gras tapestry, all intensely illuminating and easy to follow. (📞504-568-6962; http://louisia-nastatemuseum.org; 751 Chartres St; adult/student $6/5; ⏰10am-4:30pm Tue-Sun)

Ursuline Convent
HISTORIC BUILDING

7 ◎ MAP P40, E3

One of the few surviving French Colonial buildings in New Orleans, this lovely convent is worth a tour for its architectural virtues and its small museum of Catholic bric-a-brac. After a five-month voyage from Rouen, France, 12 Ursuline nuns arrived in New Orleans in 1727. The Ursuline had a mission-ary bent, but achieved their goals through advancing the literacy rate of women of all races and social levels; their school admit-ted French, Native American and African American girls. (📞504-529-3040; www.stlouiscathedral.org/convent-museum; 1112 Chartres St; adult/student $8/6; ⏰10am-4pm Mon-Fri, 9am-3pm Sat)

Gallier House Museum
HISTORIC BUILDING

8 ◎ MAP P40, E3

Many New Orleans buildings owe their existence, either directly or by design, to James Gallier Sr and Jr, who added Greek Revivalist, British and American accents to the Quarter's French, Spanish and Creole architectural mélange. In 1857, Gallier Jr began work on this town house, which incorporates all of the above elements. The period furniture is lovely; not so much are the intact slave quarters out back – once you see these, you'll recognize them throughout the French Quarter. (📞504-274-0746; www.hgghh.org; 1132 Royal St; adult/student & senior $15/12, combined with Hermann-Grima House $25/20; ⏰tours hourly 10am-3pm Mon, Tue, Thu & Fri, noon-3pm Sat)

Eating

Bayona
LOUISIANAN $$$

9 ✕ MAP P40, A5

Bayona is one of our favorite splurges in the Quarter, and a pio-neer of the slow-food movement. It's classy but unpretentious, an all-round fine spot for a meal. The menu changes regularly, but expect fresh fish, fowl and game, prepared in a way that comes off as elegant and deeply cozy at the same time. (📞504-525-4455; www.bayona.com; 430 Dauphine St; mains $28-33; ⏰11:30am-1:30pm Wed-Sat, plus 6-9pm Mon-Thu, 5:30-10pm Fri & Sat; 🧸)

Galatoire's

CREOLE $$$

10 ⊗ MAP P40, A7

Friday lunchtime is the best time to visit this revered New Orleans institution for its traditional Creole cuisine. That's when local ladies in big hats and gloves and men wearing bowties (without irony) buy copious bottles of champagne, gossip to high hell and have eight-hour boozy lunches that, in their way, have been going on forever. You will need to dress the part; jackets are a must for men. (🎫 504-525-2021; www.galatoires.com; 209 Bourbon St; mains $20-44; 🕚 11:30am-10pm Tue-Sat, from noon Sun)

Coop's Place

CAJUN $$

11 ⊗ MAP P40, E3

Coop's is an authentic Cajun dive, but more rocked out. Make no mistake: it can be grotty and chaotic, the servers have attitude and the layout is annoying. But it's worth it for the food: rabbit jambalaya or chicken with shrimp and tasso (smoked ham) in a cream sauce. No patrons under 21. (🎫 504-525-9053; www.coopsplace. net; 1109 Decatur St; mains $10-20; 🕚 11am-midnight Sun-Thu, to 1am Fri & Sat)

SoBou

AMERICAN $$$

12 ⊗ MAP P40, B7

The name means 'South of Bourbon'. And the food? Hard to pin down, but uniformly excellent.

Ursuline Convent

JIAWANGKUN/SHUTTERSTOCK ©

The chefs play with a concept that mixes Louisiana indulgence with eccentricities: sweet-potato beignets slathered with duck gravy and chicory-coffee glaze – mmmm! The menu changes seasonally, but it's always solid, as is the innovative cocktail bar. (☑504-552-4095; www.sobounola.com; 310 Chartres St; mains $17-52; ⏰7am-10pm)

Sylvain
LOUISIANAN $$

13 ✖ MAP P40, C5

This rustic yet elegant gastropub draws inspiration from the dedication to local ingredients demonstrated by expert chefs. The menu changes often, but the focus is Southern haute cuisine, burgers, fish, ribs and the like – combined with craft cocktails with inventive names such as 'Bang for the Buck' and 'Alexander Hamilton'. (☑504-265-8123; www.sylvainnola.com; 625 Chartres St; mains $14-29; ⏰5:30-11pm Sun-Thu, to midnight Fri & Sat, 11:30am-2:30pm Fri-Sun)

Eat New Orleans
CREOLE $$

14 ✖ MAP P40, C3

Eat dishes out neo-Creole cuisine that has become immensely popular with locals; when a New Orleanian is willing to brave French Quarter parking for pork and mustard greens or stuffed peppers, you know something good's going on. Brunch is special, with highlights such as fried chicken and gravy with eggs. Rare as the unicorn in NOLA, this spot allows BYOB. (☑504-522-7222; http://eatnola.com; 900 Dumaine St; mains $13-27; ⏰11am-2pm Tue-Fri, 5:30-10pm Tue-Sat, brunch 9am-2pm Sat & Sun; ✖)

Mister Gregory's
FRENCH $

15 ✖ MAP P40, B3

That the French expat community of New Orleans regularly makes its way to Mister Gregory's should tell you something about the quality of this bistro's baguettes and sandwiches. This no-frills lunch and breakfast spot specializes in deli baguettes, plus it does a mean line of croque-style sandwiches (ie with melted cheese and béchamel on top), salads and waffles. (☑504-407-3780; www.mistergregorys.com; 806 N Rampart St; mains $5-13; ⏰9am-4pm; ✖)

Croissant D'Or Patisserie
BAKERY $

16 ✖ MAP P40, E3

Bring a paper, order coffee and a croissant – or a tart, quiche or sandwich topped with béchamel sauce – and bliss out. Check out the tiled sign on the threshold that says 'ladies entrance' – a holdover from earlier days. While the coffee is bland, the pastries are perfect, and the shop is well-lit, friendly and clean. (☑504-524-4663; www.croissantdornola.com; 615-617 Ursulines Ave; mains $3-7; ⏰6:30am-3pm Wed-Mon)

Green Goddess
FUSION $$

17 MAP P40, B7

Who serves South Indian pancakes and tamarind shrimp? Alongside smoked duck and (oh, man) truffle grits? Green Goddess, that's who. The Goddess combines a playful attitude to preparation with a world traveler's perspective on ingredient sourcing and a workman's ethic when it comes to actually cooking the stuff. No reservations accepted. (504-301-3347; www.greengoddessrestaurant.com; 307 Exchange Pl, mains $12-20; 11am-9pm Wed-Sun;)

Café Amelie
FRENCH $$

18 MAP P40, D4

We wax rhapsodic over the Quarter's beautiful backyard gardens, and Amelie's, much beloved by locals, takes the cake. An alfresco restaurant tucked behind an old carriage house and surrounded by high brick walls and shady trees, this is a supremely romantic dining spot. Fresh seafood and local produce are the basis of a modest, ever-changing menu. (504-412-8965; www.cafeamelie.com; 912 Royal St; mains $15-29; 11am-3pm Wed-Sun, 5-9pm Wed, Thu & Sun, to 10pm Fri & Sat)

Court of the Two Sisters
CREOLE $$$

19 MAP P40, C5

The Court regularly ranks in 'best place for brunch in New Orleans' lists, a standing that can be attributed to its setting as much as its food. The latter is a circus of Creole omelets, Cajun pasta salads, grillades, fruits, meats and fruity cocktails; the former is an enchanting Creole garden filled with sugar-scented warm air with soft jazz playing. (504-522-7261; www.courtoftwosisters.com; 613 Royal St; mains $18-37, brunch $32; 9am-3pm & 5:30-10pm)

Stanley
CREOLE $

20 MAP P40, D5

While sandwiches and other lunchy things are available at Stanley, we're all about the breakfast. Bananas Foster French toast and fluffy pancakes provide the sweet, while a Breaux Bridge Benedict with boudin (Cajun sausage) and local hollandaise does up the savory side. Either option is delicious. (504-587-0093; www.stanleyrestaurant.com; 547 St Ann St; mains $10-16; 7am-7pm)

Bourbon House
CREOLE $$$

21 MAP P40, A7

The Bourbon House is an outpost of the Brennan restaurant empire. While you'll find a nice steak and pulled pork on the menu, seafood is the specialty here. Catfish is served crusted with pecans in a rich butter sauce, while the barbecued shrimp, heavily laced with rosemary and black pepper, is absolute magic. Not surprisingly, plenty of bourbons as well. (504-522-0111; 144 Bourbon St; mains

PAGE LIGHT STUDIOS/SHUTTERSTOCK ©

Beignets, Café du Monde

$21-42; ⏱6:30am-10pm Sun-Thu, to 11pm Fri & Sat)

K-Paul's Louisiana Kitchen CAJUN $$$

23 ⊗ MAP P40, B7

This was the home base of late chef Paul Prudhomme, who was essentially responsible for putting modern Louisiana cooking on the culinary map. The kitchen's still cranking out quality: blackened twin beef tenders ($37), a signature dish, come with an incredibly rich 'debris' gravy that's been slowly cooked over a two-day period. (☎504-596-2530; www.kpauls.com; 416 Chartres St; mains $33-37; ⏱5:30-10pm Mon-Sat, 11am-2pm Thu-Sat)

Café du Monde CAFE $

23 ⊗ MAP P40, D5

Café du Monde is the most popular destination in New Orleans and, unfortunately, it often feels that way. But once you do get seated, the beignets (square, sugar-coated fritters) and chicory café au lait, served here since 1862, are decadent and delicious. Open 24 hours a day, seven days a week – the cafe only closes for Christmas Day. (☎504-525-4544; www.cafedumonde.com; 800 Decatur St; beignets $3; ⏱24hr)

Central Grocery DELI $

24 ⊗ MAP P40, E4

There are a few New Orleans names inextricably linked to a

certain dish, and Central Grocery is the word-association winner for the *muffuletta*. That's pronounced 'muffa-lotta', and the name about sums it up: your mouth will be muffled by a hell of a lotta sandwich, stuffed with meat, cheese and sharp olive salad. (📞504-523-1620; 923 Decatur St; sandwiches $12-23; ⏱9am-5pm)

Drinking

Bar Tonique COCKTAIL BAR

25 🚇 MAP P40, B3

Providing shelter from sobriety since 08/08/08, Tonique is a bartender's bar. Seriously, on a Sunday night, when the weekend rush is over, we've seen no fewer than three of the city's top bartenders arrive here to unwind. This gem mixes some of the best drinks in the city, offering a spirits menu as long as a Tolstoy novel. (📞504-324-6045; www.bartonique.com; 820 N Rampart St; ⏱noon-2am)

Tiki Tolteca BAR

26 🚇 MAP P40, C8

Though this great tiki bar shares the block with another tiki-themed powerhouse, **Latitude 29** (📞504-609-3811; http://latitude29nola.com; 321 N Peters St; ⏱3-11pm Sun-Thu, 1pm-midnight Fri & Sat), they're as different as Tahiti and Hawaii. Here you'll find a small, intimate bar, where it's easy to chat and make new friends, and some impressive drinks – which pack a punch. There's a daily happy hour (from opening until 7pm). The entrance

is around the corner on Bienville. (http://tikitolteca.com; 301 N Peters St; ⏱5-11pm Mon-Thu, noon-2am Fri & Sat, noon-11pm Sun)

French 75 BAR

27 🚇 MAP P40, A6

This spot is all wood and patrician accents, but the staff is friendly and down to earth. They'll mix high-quality drinks that will make you feel (a) like the star of your own Tennessee Williams play about decadent Southern aristocracy and (b) blissfully drunk. Definitely dress up for this ritzy place, which is perfect after a dinner at **Arnaud's** (📞504-523-5433; www.arnauds.com; 813 Bienville St; mains $26-42; ⏱6-10pm Mon-Sat, 10am-2:30pm & 6-10pm Sun). (📞504-523-5433; www.arnaudsrestaurant.com/bars/french-75; 813 Bienville St; ⏱5:30-11:30pm Sun-Thu, to 12:30am Fri & Sat)

Patrick's Bar Vin WINE BAR

28 🚇 MAP P40, A7

With its carpets, plush chairs, nooks and shelves upon shelves of wine, you'll feel like you're visiting a rich friend's house when you have a glass or two here. Along with its own extensive collection, Patrick's Bar Vin offers a limited number of personal, temperature-controlled wine lockers to keep your precious bottles safely stored. (📞504-200-3180; http://patricksbarvin.com; 730 Bienville St; ⏱4pm-midnight Mon-Thu, noon-1am Fri, 2pm-1am Sat, 2pm-midnight Sun)

The Emperor's Aborted Exile

The Napoleon House bar has a colorful connection to its namesake. After Waterloo and the subsequent banishment of the French emperor to St Helena, a band of loyal New Orleanians reputedly plotted to rescue Napoleon and set him up in this building's 3rd-floor digs. Alas, Napoleon croaked mere days before the plan was to become action. It seems a stretch to imagine Bonaparte whiling away his last days in this pleasant home, telling tall tales about conquering Europe.

Cane & Table   COCKTAIL BAR

29 🚇 MAP P40, E3

One of the classier venues in this part of the Quarter, the Cane & Table – with its romantically faded interior and Mediterranean-style outdoor courtyard – is so stunning it's hard to knock. The drinks are fun, playful and inventive, some with a tiki-type vibe. And did we mention they're tasty, too? (📞504-581-1112; www.caneandtablenola.com; 1113 Decatur St; ⏰3pm-midnight Mon-Thu, to 1am Fri & Sat)

Carousel Bar   BAR

30 🚇 MAP P40, A7

At this smart-looking spot inside the historic Hotel Monteleone, you'll find a revolving circular bar, canopied by the top hat of the 1904 World's Fair carousel, adorned with running lights, hand-painted figures and gilded mirrors. In 15 minutes the 25-seat bar completes a full revolution. A top spot for a tipple you'll remember for a while. Careful on your way out. (📞504-523-3341; http://hotel-monteleone.com/entertainment; 214 Royal St; ⏰11am-midnight Sun-Thu, to 1am Fri & Sat)

Lafitte's Blacksmith Shop   BAR

31 🚇 MAP P40, C3

This gutted brick cottage claims to be the country's oldest operating bar – it certainly is the oldest in the South, and one of the most atmospheric in the Quarter. Rumors suggest it was once the workshop of pirate Jean Lafitte and his brother Pierre. Whether true or not (historical records suggest not), the house dates to the 18th century. (📞504-593-9761; www.lafittesblacksmithshop.com; 941 Bourbon St; ⏰10:30am-3am Sun-Thu, to 4am Fri & Sat)

Napoleon House   BAR

32 🚇 MAP P40, C6

By all appearances, the Napoleon House's stuccoed walls haven't received so much as a dab of paint since the place opened in 1805. The diffused glow pouring through open doors and windows in the afternoon draws out the room's gorgeous patina. The bar serves a good range of stiff mixed drinks, cold beer, and a popular Pimm's Cup. (504-524-9752; www.napoleonhouse.com; 500 Chartres St; 11am-10pm Sun-Thu, to 11pm Fri & Sat)

Black Penny BAR

33 MAP P40, A3

Run by the folks from nearby Bar Tonique, this spot focuses on great brews, though you can get a fine cocktail if you so desire. Even folks without much taste for traditional beer can find a tipple they might like (such as fruit or ginger beers), and the comfy booths make it easier to talk with friends. (504-304-4770; www.facebook.com/BlackPennyNola; 700 N Rampart St; noon-4am)

Pat O'Brien's BAR

34 MAP P40, C5

Yes, it's a campy tourist trap, but Pat O'Brien's has genuine atmosphere and history, and where else can you see copper-clad steampunk-esque dueling pianos playing different versions of '80s Billy Joel hits? The courtyard, lit by flaming fountains, is genuinely lovely, but folks mainly pack in for their Hurricanes, a blend of rum, juice and grenadine. (504-525-4823; www.patobriens.com; 718 St Peter St; noon-2am Mon-Thu, 10am-4am Fri-Sun)

Molly's at the Market IRISH PUB

35 MAP P40, E3

A cop, a reporter and a tourist walk into a bar. That's not a joke,

just a good description of the eclectic clientele you get at this excellent neighborhood bar. It's also the home of a fat cat (Mr Wu), some kicking Irish coffee and an urn containing the ashes of its founder. (504-525-5169; www.mollysatthemarket.net; 1107 Decatur St; 10am-6am)

Spitfire Coffee COFFEE

36 MAP P40, C5

This spot specializes in pour-over coffee and espresso drinks ($1.50 to $4.50). It serves some of the Quarter's strongest coffee, eschewing the usual amounts of milk. It's a take-out spot, so grab that coffee, wander over to nearby Jackson Sq, and fuel up for some caffeine-powered sightseeing. The Hellfire Mocha ($5.50) is a fiery concoction any chili addict should try. (www.spitfirecoffee.com; 627 St Peter St; 8am-8pm)

Deja Vu BAR

37 MAP P40, A6

Deja Vu is everything a neighborhood bar should be: mainly, it's there when you are, be that 7:30am or midnight. Open 24/7, Deja Vu has cheap beers, decent cocktails, a friendly vibe, super-sweet bartenders, and even food. Nothing hoity-toity here, just a good local bar. Did we mention that it's open 24 hours? (504-523-1931; http://dejavunola.com; 400 Dauphine St; 24hr)

Chart Room
BAR

38 🕒 MAP P40, B7

The Chart Room is simply a great bar. There's a historical patina on the walls, outdoor seating for people-watching and a cast of characters plucked from Fellini's 8½ casting call. You may even meet Pocahontas. Or someone who believes he is her. (📞504-522-1708; 300 Chartres St; 🕐11am-4am)

Bourbon Pub & Parade
GAY

39 🕒 MAP P40, C4

The Bourbon is the heart of New Orleans' gay nightlife and party scene. Many of the events that pepper the city's gay calendar either begin, end or are conducted here; during **Southern Decadence** (www.southerndecadence.net; 🕐1st weekend Sep), in particular, this is the place to be. Ladies are welcome, but this is pretty much a bar for the boys. (📞504-529-2107; www.bourbonpub.com; 801 Bourbon St; 🕐10am-3am Sun-Thu, 24hr Fri & Sat)

Entertainment

Fritzel's European Jazz Pub
JAZZ

40 ⭐ MAP P40, C4

There's no cover charge at this awesome venue for live jazz, which is so small that you really can't have a bad seat. The seating is kind of rustic: benches and chairs so tightly packed that you'll be apologizing for disturbing people each time you go to the bathroom.

But the music is great, everything New Orleans jazz should be. (📞504-586-4800; www.fritzelsjazz. net; 733 Bourbon St; 🕐noon-midnight Sun-Thu, to 2am Fri & Sat)

Preservation Hall
JAZZ

41 ⭐ MAP P40, C5

Preservation Hall, housed in a former art gallery dating from 1803, is one of New Orleans' most storied live-music venues. The resident performers, the Preservation Hall Jazz Band, are ludicrously talented, and regularly tour the world. 'The Hall' dates from 1961, when Barbara Reid and Grayson 'Ken' Mills formed the Society for the Preservation of New Orleans Jazz. (📞504-522-2841; www.preservationhall.com; 726 St Peter St; cover Sun-Thu $15, Fri & Sat $20, reserved seats Sun-Thu $35-45, Fri & Sat $40-50; 🕐showtimes 8pm, 9pm & 10pm, also 5pm & 6pm Thu-Sun)

Fleur de Tease
DANCE

If you're in the mood for something a bit risqué, we'd recommend catching this burlesque show (see 42 ⭐ Map p40, C5). These talented ladies, many of whom claim professional dance backgrounds, blend vintage vibe with a modern, in-your-face post-feminist sexuality that is pretty enticing for both men and women. They perform all over town, including at One Eyed Jacks every other Sunday. (📞504-975-1245; http://fleurdetease.com)

One Eyed Jacks
LIVE MUSIC

42 ⭐ MAP P40, C5

If you've been thinking, 'I could use a night at a bar that feels like a 19th-century bordello managed by Johnny Rotten,' you're in luck. Jacks is a great venue; there's a sense that dangerous women in corsets, men with Mohawks and an army of bohemians with absinthe bottles would come charging out at any moment. The musical acts are consistently good. (📞504-569-8361; www. oneeyedjacks.net; 615 Toulouse St; cover $10-25)

Palm Court Jazz Café
JAZZ

43 ⭐ MAP P40, F3

Fans of trad jazz who want to hang out with a mature crowd should head to this supper-club venue. Palm Court is a roomy spot that has a consistently good lineup of local legends; you really can't go wrong if you're a jazz fan. Shows start at 8pm. (📞504-525-0200; www. palmcourtjazzcafe.com; 1204 Decatur St; cover around $5; ⏱7-11pm Wed-Sun)

Shopping

Fifi Mahony's
COSMETICS

44 🔒 MAP P40, D3

New Orleans is the most costume-crazy city in the USA, and Fifi Mahony's is the place to go to don a wig. There's a stunning selection of hairpieces here that runs the gamut from the glittered to the

Rev Zombie's House of Voodoo (p55)

bechived, presented in a veritable rainbow of colors. An on-site beauty salon and sassy staff round out the experience. (📞504-525-4343; 934 Royal St; ⏱noon-6pm Sun-Wed, 11am-7pm Thu-Sat)

MS Rau Antiques
ANTIQUES

45 🔒 MAP P40, C5

With a massive 30,000-sq-ft showroom, and after a century of doing business, MS Rau ranks among New Orleans' most venerated dealers of antiques. It's all a bit serious – these are the sort of frosty antiques that require their own insurance policies – but it's a family business and the professional salespeople are warm and approachable. (📞504-523-5660;

www.rauantiques.com; 630 Royal St; ⏰9am-5:15pm Mon-Sat)

SecondLine Art & Antiques ARTS & CRAFTS

46 🔒 MAP P40, F3

Get unique crafts, art, antiques and souvenirs at this co-op, which includes an indoor gallery space and a courtyard night market outside. Meet the artists and know that your purchase goes directly to the creators themselves. Everything from moose heads to jewelry to votive candles might be found. Come in and browse! (📞504-875-1924; www.secondlinenola.com; 1209 Decatur; ⏰8am-8pm Sun-Wed, to 10pm Thu, to midnight Fri & Sat, market 5pm-1am Thu-Mon)

Little Toy Shop GIFTS & SOUVENIRS

47 🔒 MAP P40, D5

Packed nearly floor to ceiling with toys and gifts for the younger set, this bustling shop has just about anything your kids, nieces, nephews or other such relatives might want. Choose between books, games, jokes, string dolls, voodoo and magic sets, stuffed animals and pet rocks. (📞504-523-1770; http://littletoyshops.com; 513 St Ann St; ⏰8:30am-8:30pm)

Hové Parfumeur COSMETICS

48 🔒 MAP P40, C6

Grassy vetiver, bittersweet orange blossoms, spicy ginger – New Orleans' exotic flora has graciously lent its scents to Hové's house-made perfumes for almost a century. In its 90th year, female-owned and -operated for more than four generations, it's an inspiring spot that will leave your head swirling with images of the Vieux Carré's magnificent past. (📞504-525-7827; www.hoveparfumeur.com; 434 Chartres St; ⏰10am-6pm Mon-Sat, from 11am Sun)

Boutique du Vampyre GIFTS & SOUVENIRS

49 🔒 MAP P40, C4

This dungeon-esque store stocks all kinds of vampire-themed gifts. Come here for books, curses, spells, souvenirs and witty banter with the awesome clerks who oversee this curious crypt. Among the items is a deck of tarot cards with truly surreal, somewhat disturbing artwork. If your fangs have chipped, their on-call fangsmith can even shape you a new custom pair. (📞504-561-8267; www.feelthebite.com; 709 St Ann St; ⏰10am-9pm)

Lucullus ANTIQUES

50 🔒 MAP P40, C6

Peeking in the window, you'll see a battery of ancient copper pots that appear to have generations of dents tinkered out of their bottoms. Owner Patrick Dunne is an advocate of using, not merely collecting, antiques. Follow his advice and add more ritual and elegance to your life with an antique café au lait bowl or an absinthe spoon. (📞504-528-9620;

http://lucullusantiques.com; 610 Chartres St; ⏰9am-5pm Mon-Sat)

Faulkner House Books   BOOKS

51 🔒 MAP P40, C5

The erudite owner of this former residence of author William Faulkner sells rare first editions and new titles in an airy, elegant and charming independent bookshop. And, yes, there are a number of Faulkner titles on sale as well. (☎504-524-2940; www.faulknerhousebooks.com; 624 Pirate Alley; ⏰10am-5pm)

French Quarter Postal Emporium   GIFTS & SOUVENIRS

52 🔒 MAP P40, D3

The wide variety of gifts here ranges from raunchy Bourbon St tropes (gag gifts, wince-worthy quips on T-shirts and mugs) to the genuinely beautiful, such as art, crafts and other souvenirs. (☎504-525-6651; www.frenchquarterpostal.net; 1000 Bourbon St; ⏰9am-6pm Mon-Fri, 10am-3pm Sat)

Rev Zombie's House of Voodoo   GIFTS & SOUVENIRS

53 🔒 MAP P40, C5

Step inside and you'll see this is one religious store that's not bent on snuffing out the party. An altar at the entry includes a serious request that you not take photos, but then comes a truly splendiferous display of plaster-of-Paris statuettes imported from the Santería realms of Brazil. All are fun and charming; many are simply beautiful. (☎504-486-6366; www.voodooneworleans.com; 723 St Peter St; ⏰10am-11:30pm Sun-Thu, to 1:30am Fri & Sat)

Od Aomo   CLOTHING

54 🔒 MAP P40, D4

Dr Sophia Aomo Omoro has worn many hats in her life: runway model, surgeon, philanthropist and now proprietor of a high-end fashion boutique. All of the clothes under her label are made in her native Kenya, where she is dedicated to providing increased employment. Her style sits at a hip intersection of ethnic patterns and contemporary chic. (☎504-460-5730; www.odaomo.com; 839 Chartres St; ⏰10am-6pm Mon-Sat, to 5pm Sun)

Maskarade   GIFTS & SOUVENIRS

55 🔒 MAP P40, C4

Do not confuse this with a joke shop or a spot for those Groucho Marx nose 'n' glasses. Decades old, this place deals in high-quality masks by local and international artisans. The selection includes everything from classic *commedia dell'arte* masks from Venice to masks worn by the Cirque du Soleil. Think hang-on-the-wall art, not wear-for-Mardi-Gras. (☎504-568-1018; www.themaskstore.com; 630 St Ann St; ⏰10am-5pm)

Explore
Faubourg Marigny & Bywater

Just downriver from the French Quarter, the Marigny and Bywater are both Creole faubourgs (literally 'suburbs,' although 'neighborhood' is more accurate in spirit). They were situated at the edge of gentrification, and attracted a glut of artists and creative types, as such areas are wont to do. While gentrification has firmly set in, these remain fascinating, beautiful neighborhoods – the homes are bright, painted like so many rows of pastel fruit, and plenty of oddballs still call this home.

You can easily explore the Marigny or Bywater on foot or with two wheels, eating, drinking and shopping wherever the spirit moves you. When you're tired of buildings, food or booze, enjoy the Mississippi from Crescent Park (p61). In the evening, head out to catch music or theater along St Claude Ave or on Frenchmen St.

Getting There & Around

🚌 Bus 5 runs into the heart of Marigny and Bywater.

🚗 If you're driving, note that on weekend nights the streets get packed around Frenchmen St.

🚲 It's an easy bike ride out here. If you're heading to Bywater, ride through Crescent Park, but note the access point on St Peters St is by elevator.

Neighborhood Map on p60

Southern-style home, Faubourg Marigny FOTOLUMINATE LLC/SHUTTERSTOCK

Walking Tour 🚶

A Night of Jazz & Live Music

Frenchmen St is often sold as a 'locals' Bourbon St,' but these days, it attracts just as many tourists as residents. Still, this is the site of many a New Orleanians' date night, friends' night out, etc. Why? Because this is a town that loves live music, and this is still the best concentration of music in the city.

Walk Facts

Start Dragon's Den
End Kajun's
Length 0.8 miles; 1½ hours

❶ Dragon's Den

When it comes to rock, ska, punk, drum and bass, dubstep and hip-hop, **Dragon's Den** (☎504-940-5546; www.dragonsdennola. com; 435 Esplanade Ave; cover $5-10; ⊙7pm-late) consistently hosts some great acts. It has more grit and more millennials than the average Frenchmen St hangout.

❷ Maison

Enter Marigny proper via the live music strip of Frenchmen St. Get your evening started at Maison (p69); it's one of the fancier Frenchmen spots and has a good mix of acts. Try one of the special house vodkas and enjoy the music, which starts on the early side.

❸ Cafe Negril

When you spin the Frenchmen St musical wheel, Cafe Negril (p69) is the stop for reggae, blues, Latin and world music. If you're craving that sort of groove, roll on in.

❹ People-Watching on Frenchmen St

Frenchmen St is a consistently good spot for people-watching, though it can be a little rowdy on weekends. The main strip is only three blocks long, but you can view a lifetime's worth of the human tapestry on any given night: buskers, poets for hire, hustlers, the hustled, the costumed and the drunken revellers.

❺ Spotted Cat

It's packed, it's loud, it's sweaty and the sight lines can be bad, but the Cat (p67) is still one of the finest music clubs in town. It feels raw, the music is excellent, and in between the perspiration and the stale booze is the sense that you're on the doorstep of musical greatness.

❻ Phoenix Bar

It's time to head toward St Claude Ave but don't think of going all the way over there without a refueling go-cup (takeaway) drink! I lead to Phoenix Bar (p69), a fantastic gay bar where the leather-and-denim community meets. Much more of a locals' scene than similar spots in the Quarter.

❼ Gene's

You've probably had a bit to eat and drink by now, but a stop at Gene's (p65), a 24-hour pink palace, is worthwhile for a finely mixed daiquiri and a mean hot sausage po'boy.

❽ St Claude Square

At St Claude Ave and Marigny St, you'll find venues that cater to a New Orleans crowd that runs from university students to crust punks and beyond. Acts here have a similarly broad scope. This is where you can access the music that the city's younger tastemakers are listening to – and afterward, you can karaoke like a wild one at Kajun's (p68).

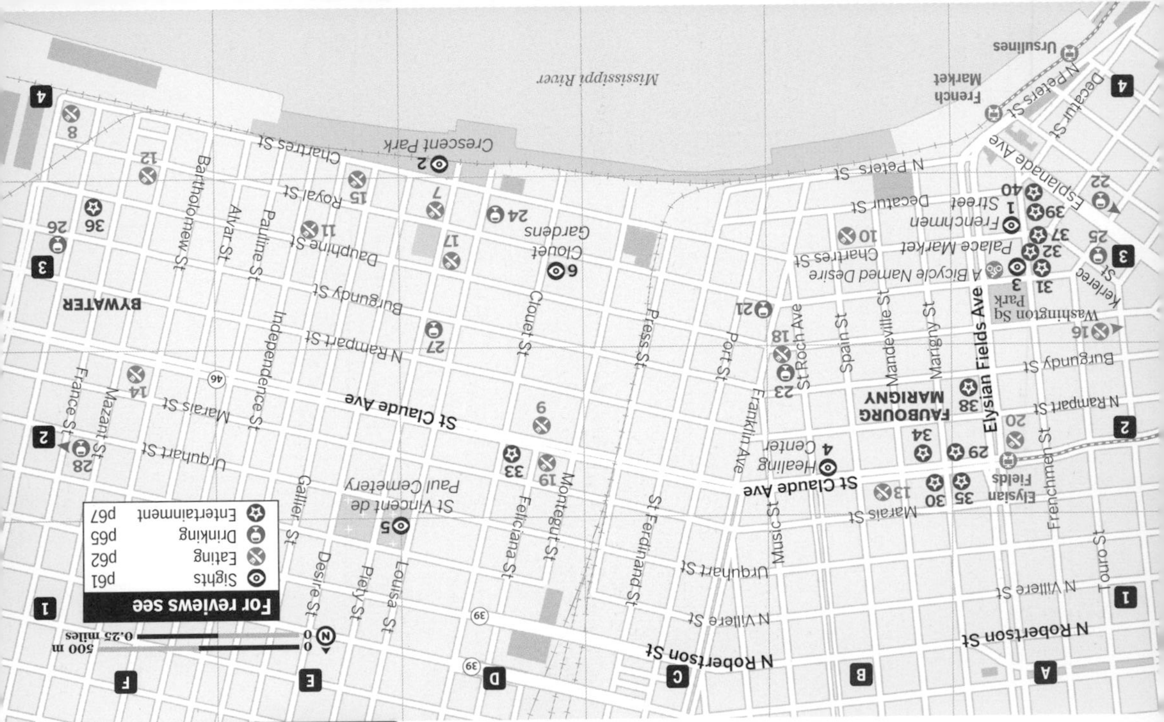

Faubourg Marigny & Bywater

For reviews see

◎ Sights p61
⊗ Eating p62
⊗ Drinking p65
⊗ Entertainment p67

500 m
0.25 miles

BYWATER

FAUBOURG MARIGNY

Mississippi River

Crescent Park

French Market

St Vincent de Paul Cemetery

St Claude Ave

Healing Center

A Bicycle Named Desire

Palace Market
Frenchmen Street

Washington Sq Park

Elysian Fields

Clouet Gardens

Streets: N Robertson St, N Villere St, N Rampart St, Burgundy St, Dauphine St, Royal St, Chartres St, Decatur St, N Peters St, Esplanade Ave, Frenchmen St, Elysian Fields Ave, Marigny St, Mandeville St, Spain St, St Roch Ave, St Ferdinand St, Press St, Montegut St, Clouet St, Louisa St, Piety St, Desire St, Galler St, Independence St, Pauline St, Alvar St, Bartholomew St, Mazant St, France St, Franklin Ave, Port St, Music St, Urquhart St, Marais St, St Claude Ave, Feliciana St, Kerlerec St, Touro St, Ursulines, N Peters St, Decatur St, St Peters St

Crescent Park

Sights

Frenchmen Street

STREET

1 ⊙ MAP P60, A3

The 'locals' Bourbon St' is how Frenchmen St is usually described to those who want to know where New Orleanians listen to music. The predictable result? Frenchmen St is now packed with out-of-towners each weekend. Still, it's a ton of fun, especially on weekdays when the crowds thin out but music still plays. Bars and clubs are arrayed back to back for several city blocks in one of the best concentrations of live-music venues in the country. (from Esplanade Ave to Royal St)

Crescent Park

PARK

2 ⊙ MAP P60, D4

This waterfront park is our favorite spot in the city for taking in the Mississippi. Enter over the enormous arch at Piety and Chartres Sts, or at the steps at Marigny and N Peters Sts, and watch the fog blanket the nearby skyline. A promenade meanders past an angular metal-and-concrete conceptual 'wharf' (placed next to the burned remains of the former commercial wharf). A dog park is located near the Mazant St entrance. (☏504-636-6400; www.crescentparknola.org; Piety, Chartres & Mazant Sts; ⊙6am-7:30pm; ⊉🚻🐕)

Palace Market

MARKET

3 ⊙ MAP P60, A3

Independent artists and artisans line this alleyway market, which has built a reputation as one of the better spots in town to find a unique gift to take home as your New Orleans souvenir. The selections include T-shirts with clever New Orleans puns, handcrafted jewelry, trinkets and a nice selection of prints and original artwork. (☏504-249-9003; www.palacemarketnola.com; 619 Frenchmen St; ⊙10pm-1am)

Healing Center

MARKET

4 ⊙ MAP P60, B2

The bright-orange Healing Center is a sort of warehouse of all things organic, spiritual, New Age and conscious-raising. Inside, you'll find yoga studios, performance spaces, a sustainable food co-op, and a central entrance hall that houses large voodoo shrines that are utilized by local adherents of the religion. (☏504-940-1130; www.neworleanshealingcenter.org; 2372 St Claude Ave; ⊙varies by store; ⊉)

St Vincent de Paul Cemetery

CEMETERY

5 ⊙ MAP P60, E1

As New Orleans cemeteries go, this one feels completely off the tourist radar. And yet, it's as atmospheric and gloomy as any other 'city of the dead.' Be on the lookout for inscriptions written in French and a slew of immigrant names encompassing émigrés from across Europe. Take a taxi or drive out here. (1401 Louisa St; ⏰8am-3:30pm)

Clouet Gardens PARK

6 ⊙ MAP P60, D3

This formerly empty lot has been transformed by its Bywater neighbors into a neat little park filled with murals and generally appealing weirdness. Performances, concerts and neighborhood get-togethers are frequently held here, and it's a favorite with local families. (707 Clouet St; ⏰sunrise-sunset; 👬👶)

Eating

Pizza Delicious ITALIAN $

7 ✖ MAP P60, D3

The thin-crust pies here are done New York–style and taste great. The preparation is simple, but the ingredients are fresh and consistently top-notch. An easy, family-friendly ambience makes for a lovely spot for a casual dinner, and it serves good beer too if you're in the mood. Vegan pizzas are available. The outdoor area is pet-friendly. (📞504-676-8482; www.pizzadelicious.com; 617 Piety St; pizza by slice from $2.25, whole pie from $15; ⏰11am-11pm Tue-Sun; 🖊👬👶)

Bacchanal AMERICAN $$

8 ✖ MAP P60, F4

From the outside, Bacchanal looks like a leaning Bywater shack; inside

are racks of wine and stinky-but-sexy cheese. Musicians play in the garden, while cooks dispense delicious meals on paper plates from the kitchen in the back; on any given day you may try chorizo-stuffed dates or seared diver scallops that will blow your gastronomic mind. (📞504-948-9111; www.bacchanalwine.com; 600 Poland Ave; mains $8-21, cheese from $6; ⏰11am-midnight Sun-Thu, to 1am Fri & Sat)

Red's Chinese CHINESE $

9 ✖ MAP P60, D2

Red's has upped the Chinese cuisine game in New Orleans in a big way. The chefs aren't afraid to add lashings of Louisiana flavor, yet this isn't what we'd call 'fusion' cuisine. The food is grounded deeply in spicy Szechuan flavors, which pairs well with the occasional dash of cayenne. (📞504-304-6030; www.redschinese.com; 3048 St Claude Ave; mains $5-18; ⏰noon-11pm; 🖊)

Cake Café & Bakery BREAKFAST $

10 ✖ MAP P60, B3

On weekend mornings the line quite literally extends out the door here. Biscuits and gravy (topped with andouille – smoked pork sausage), fried oysters and grits (seasonally available), and all the omelets are standouts. Lunch is great, too, as are the cakes (goat cheese and apple king cake!) whipped up in the back. (📞504-943-0010; www.nolacakes.com; 2440 Chartres St; mains $6.25-13; ⏰7am-3pm Wed-Mon)

Bywater Bakery
BAKERY $

11  MAP P60, E3

This bakery is doing things right. It serves breakfasts – say, shrimp and grits or biscuits and gravy – in a cup (it works!), fantastic quiches, open-faced sandwiches, and slices of some of the most drop-dead delicious cakes you've ever tried. The king cake is so addictive it should be banned. Just kidding. (504-336-3336; www.bywaterbakery.com; 3624 Dauphine St; mains $6-9, 7am-5pm;)

Joint
BARBECUE $

12 MAP P60, F4

The Joint's smoked meat has the olfactory effect of the Sirens' sweet song, pulling you, the proverbial traveling sailor, off course and into a savory meat-induced blissful death (classical Greek analogies ending now). Enjoy some ribs, pulled pork or brisket with some sweet tea in the backyard garden and learn to love life if you haven't already. (504-949-3232; www.alwayssmokin.com; 701 Mazant St; mains $7.50-18; 11:30am-10pm Mon-Sat)

Kebab
MIDDLE EASTERN $

13 MAP P60, B2

Americans are learning what Europeans and Middle Easterners have long known: when you're drunk (and, to be fair, even when sober), shaved meat or falafel served on flatbread with lots of delicious sauces and vegetables is *amazing*. Kebab has come to preach this gospel in New Orleans, and does

Bacchanal

PAGE LIGHT STUDIOS/GETTY IMAGES ©

Faubourg Marigny & Bywater Eating

so deliciously. (📞504-383-4328; www.kebabnola.com; 2315 St Claude Ave; mains $6.50-9.50; ⏱11am-11pm Sun, Mon, Wed, & Thu, to midnight Fri & Sat, closed Tue; 🖗)

Sneaky Pickle   VEGAN $

14 ❌ MAP P60, F2

This city has been sorely in need of a vegan-friendly spot that can hold its own against the city's famously meat-heavy cuisine. Enter Sneaky Pickle, a little spot on St Claude that dishes out tempeh Reubens on sourdough, beet flatbreads and a ton of unexpected, tasty specials, including one changing meat dish. (📞504-218-5651; www.yousneakypickle.com; 4017 St Claude Ave; mains $5-9.25; ⏱11am-9pm; 🖗)

Elizabeth's   CAJUN, CREOLE $$

15 ❌ MAP P60, E3

Elizabeth's is deceptively down-at-heel, but the food's as good as the best New Orleans chefs can offer. It's all friendliness, smiling sass, weird artistic edges and overindulgence on the food front. Brunch and breakfast are top draws – the praline bacon is no doubt sinful, mixing greasy salt and honeyed sweet sugar, but consider us happily banished from the Garden. (📞504-944-9272; www.elizabethsrestaurantnola.com; 601 Gallier St; mains $11-26; ⏱8am-2:30pm & 6-10pm Mon-Sat, 8am-2:30pm Sun)

Rampart Food Store   SANDWICHES $

16 ❌ MAP P60, A3

This convenience store is run by Vietnamese immigrants who know how to make some of the best, most overstuffed shrimp po'boys in New Orleans. Pass on everything else, and be prepared for long lines. (📞504-944-7777; 1700 N Rampart St; po'boys $7-11; ⏱8am-8pm Mon-Sat)

Satsuma   CAFE $

17 ❌ MAP P60, D3

With its chalkboard menu of organic soups and sandwiches, ginger limeade (seriously, this drink on a hot day is heaven), and graphic- and-pop art-decorated walls, Satsuma is hip and fun. Kids' books and indulgent staff make this an ideal spot for your children. (📞504-304-5962; www.satsumacafe.com; 3218 Dauphine St; mains $5.50-10.50; ⏱7am-5pm; 🖗👶)

Lost Love   VIETNAMESE $

18 ❌ MAP P60, B2

This divey neighborhood bar also has a Vietnamese kitchen in the back serving great pho, *banh mi* (Vietnamese po'boys) and spring rolls. Just be aware the atmosphere isn't standard Vietnamese American dive (Formica, old Republic flag, karaoke); this place is more of an inked-up hideaway. (📞504-949-2009; 2529 Dauphine St; mains $5.25-12; ⏱6pm-midnight)

PAGE LIGHT STUDIOS/GETTY IMAGES ©

d.b.a. (p68), Frenchmen St

Junction

AMERICAN $

19 MAP P60, D2

Junction takes a tight-focused approach to cuisine: it does cheeseburgers, and does them well. Variations include an Iowa burger with corn relish, blue cheese and bacon. The cheeseburgers come with hand-cut fries, and there are fine salads and wings on the menu as well. An enormous beer menu is also tempting. Junction is a 21-and-over establishment.

Note that the kitchen closes at 1:30am. (☎504-272-0205; www.junctionnola.com; 3021 St Claude Ave; mains $9-13; ⊙11am-2am)

Gene's

SANDWICHES $

20 MAP P60, A2

It's hard to miss Gene's: with its pink-and-yellow exterior, it's one of the most vividly painted buildings on Elysian Fields Ave. The hot sausage po'boy with cheese, and the fact it is served 24/7 with a free drink, is the reason you come here. (☎504-943-3861; 1040 Elysian Fields Ave; po'boys $8; ⊙24hr)

Drinking

Mimi's in the Marigny

BAR

21 MAP P60, C3

The name of this bar could justifiably change to 'Mimi's *is* the Marigny' – it's impossible to imagine the neighborhood without this institution. It's an attractively disheveled place, with comfy furniture, pool tables, an upstairs dance hall decorated like a Creole mansion gone punk, and dim brown lighting like a fantasy in sepia. The bar closes when the bartenders want it to. (☏504-872-9868; www.mimismarigny.com; 2601 Royal St; ☺3pm-late Mon-Fri, 11am-late Sat & Sun)

Buffa's BAR

22 ☎ MAP P60, A3

Buffa's wears a lot of hats. First and foremost, it's a neighborhood bar with a backroom stage that hosts the occasional band, quiz night, open-mic night and TV/movie screening. Second, it's a 24-hour spot that serves one of the best cheeseburgers in town – the Buffa burger, a half pound of char-grilled meaty perfection. (☏504-949-0038; www.buffasrestaurant.com; 1001 Esplanade Ave; ☺24hr)

Lost Love BAR

23 ☎ MAP P60, B2

Dark and sexy, Lost Love is that vampy Marigny goth or moody artist your momma told you to stay away from, mixed with a bit of blue-collar dive-bar sensibility. The drinks are cheap, the pours are strong, there are regular trivia nights, movies and TV shows are projected onto a big screen, and there's an excellent Vietnamese kitchen in the back. (☏504-949-2009; 2529 Dauphine St; ☺2pm-2am Mon-Fri, from 11am Sat & Sun)

Country Club BAR

24 ☎ MAP P60, D3

From the front, it's a well-decorated Bywater house. Walk inside and there's a restaurant, sauna, leafy patio with bar, heated outdoor pool, 25ft projector screen and a hot tub. There's a $10 towel rental fee if you want to hang out in the pool area, which is a popular carousing spot for the gay and lesbian community (all sexualities welcome). (☏504-945-0742; www.thecountryclubneworleans.com; 634 Louisa St; ☺10am-1am daily)

R Bar BAR

25 ☎ MAP P60, A3

This grotty spot seamlessly blends punk-rock sensibility with the occasional confused French Quarter tourist. Like many older New Orleans businesses, R Bar's appeal lies in its rough edges: a beer and a shot cost a few bucks, the pool tables constantly crack, the juke-box is great and everyone seems to stop by on Mardi Gras (p18) day. (☏504-948-7499; www.royalstreetinn.com; 1431 Royal St; ☺3pm-3am Sun-Thu, to 5am Fri & Sat)

BJ's BAR

26 ☎ MAP P60, F3

This Bywater dive attracts a neighborhood crowd seeking cheap beers, chilled-out banter and frequent events, from blues-rock gigs to sci-fi readings by local authors. How great is this place? Robert Plant felt the need to put on an impromptu set here when he visited town. Cash only. (www.facebook.com/bjs.bywater; 4301 Burgundy St)

Bud Rip's

BAR

27 🍴 MAP P60, D3

One of the oldest bars in Bywater (and Bywater has a lot of old bars), Bud Rip's clientele is at the junction of the old Bywater working class crowd and the new hipster kids who are moving in around them. Drinks are strong and cheap, and DJs spin on weekends. ([☎]504-945-5762; 900 Piety St; ⏰1pm-late)

Solo Espresso

CAFE

28 🍴 MAP P60, F2

This little shack serves very fine, strong, small-batch coffee, and its espresso drinks are seriously rocket-fueled and delicious. ([☎]504-408-1377; www.soloespressobar.com; 1301 Poland Ave; ⏰7am-3pm Mon-Sat, 9am-1pm Sun)

Entertainment

AllWays Lounge

THEATER, LIVE MUSIC

29 ⭐ MAP P60, A2

In a city full of funky music venues, AllWays stands out as one of the funkiest. On any given night of the week you may see experimental guitar, local theater, thrash-y rock, live comedy, burlesque and a '60s-inspired shagadelic dance party. Also, the drinks are super cheap.

A cover fee applies only during shows. ([☎]504-218-5778; www.theallwayslounge.net; 2240 St Claude Ave; cover $5-10; ⏰6pm-2am Sun-Thu, to 4am Fri & Sat)

Spotted Cat

LIVE MUSIC

The Cat (see 3 ⊙ Map p60, A3) might just be your sexy dream of a New Orleans jazz club, a thumping sweatbox where drinks are served in plastic cups, impromptu dances break out at the drop of a feathered hat and the music is always exceptional. Fair warning, though, it can get crowded. (www.spottedcatmusicclub.com; 623 Frenchmen St; cover $5-10; ⏰2pm-2am Mon-Fri, noon-2am Sat & Sun)

Hi Ho Lounge

LIVE MUSIC

30 ⭐ MAP P60, B2

Hip-hop, punk, brass bands, dance parties, live storytelling events and Mardi Gras Indians regularly pop up at Hi Ho, one of the most eclectic venues in an eclectic city. It can get pretty packed, but this remains one of the best mid-sized venues in town for a live act. May stay open later on weekends. ([☎]504-945-4446; www.hiholounge.net; 2239 St Claude Ave; ⏰5pm-1am Sun-Thu, to 3am Fri & Sat)

Snug Harbor

JAZZ

31 ⭐ MAP P60, A3

There may be bigger venues but Snug Harbor is still one of the best jazz clubs in the city. That's partly because it usually hosts doubleheaders, giving you a

The Best Place to Shout 'Stella!'

Tennessee Williams fans, listen up. The home at the center of *A Streetcar Named Desire* is at 632 Elysian Fields Ave. Currently the building houses the quintessentially New Orleans gift shop **I.J. Reilly's** (Map p60, A3; ☑504-304-7928; www.facebook.com/I.J.Reillys; 632 Elysian Fields Ave; ☺10am-5pm Thu-Mon, 9am-4pm Wed) and the bicycle rental outfit **A Bicycle Named Desire** (☑504-345-8966; http://abicyclenameddesire.com; 4hr/8hr/24hr rental $20/25/35, per additional day $25; ☺10am-5pm Wed-Mon) – of course.

good dose of variety, and partly because the talent is kept to an admirable mix of reliable legends and hot up-and-comers; in the course of one night you'll likely witness both. (☑504-949-0696; www.snugjazz.com; 626 Frenchmen St; cover $10-20; ☺shows at 8 & 10pm)

d.b.a.
LIVE MUSIC

32 ⭐ MAP P60, A3

Swank d.b.a. consistently schedules some of the best live-music events in town. Listening to John Boutté's sweet tenor is one of the best beginnings to a night in New Orleans. Brass bands, rock

shows, blues – everything plays here. Plus, there's an amazing beer selection. (☑504-942-3731; www.dbaneworleans.com; 618 Frenchmen St; cover $10-15; ☺4pm-5am; 🛜)

Saturn Bar
LIVE MUSIC

33 ⭐ MAP P60, D2

In the solar system of New Orleans bars, Saturn is planet odd. Originally it was an eclectic neighborhood bar where regulars appreciated the outsider art, leopard-skin furniture and a general, genuinely unique aesthetic. Today the old punks and new scenesters are united by neon-lighting fixtures, flashy gambling machines and great live music. There is no cover charge on most nights. (☑504-949-7532; 3067 St Claude Ave; cover $5; ☺7pm-late)

Kajun's Pub
KARAOKE

34 ⭐ MAP P60, B2

Kajun's is guaranteed for a good cast of characters. This bar is technically a live-music venue too...if you count karaoke as live music. In any case, the karaoke is awesome (sometimes awesomely bad, sometimes surprisingly good) and the beer flows 24/7. Many people pass a night here, stumble into the morning light and wonder what they've done with their lives. (☑504-947-3735; www.kajunpub.com; 2256 St Claude Ave; admission free; ☺24hr)

Siberia

LIVE MUSIC

35 ⭐ MAP P60, A2

There's always an interesting crowd in Siberia, which hosts everything from punk rock to singer-songwriter nights and from heavy metal to bounce shows. The on-site Eastern European–themed restaurant, **Kukhnya** (mains $5.50-10; ⏰4pm-midnight; 🖋), satisfies any cravings you may have for blinis and burgers. (📞504-265-8855; www.siberianola.com; 2227 St Claude Ave; cover $5-10; ⏰4pm-late)

Vaughan's

LIVE MUSIC

36 ⭐ MAP P60, F3

On most nights of the week this is a Bywater dive, but on Thursdays regular live music brings the house down. As small, intimate venues go, this can't be beat. It also hosts frequent drag shows and neighborhood parties. (📞504-947-5562; 800 Lesseps St; cover $5-15; ⏰noon-late)

Cafe Negril

LIVE MUSIC

37 ⭐ MAP P60, A3

When you give the Frenchmen St musical wheel a spin, Negril is the stop for reggae, blues, Latin and world music. So if you're craving that sort of thing, and the dancing that goes with it (this is definitely one of the 'dancier' clubs on Frenchmen), head on in. (📞504-383-5131; 606 Frenchmen St; cover $5; ⏰6pm-2am Sun-Thu, from 4pm Fri & Sat)

Phoenix Bar

GAY

38 ⭐ MAP P60, A2

This is where the leather-and-denim community meets to rub each other's stubble. Much more of a locals' scene than similar spots in the Quarter. (📞504-945-9264; www.phoenixbarnola.com; 941 Elysian Fields Ave; ⏰11am-midnight Mon-Fri, noon-2am Sat & Sun)

Blue Nile

LIVE MUSIC

39 ⭐ MAP P60, A3

Hip-hop, reggae, jazz, soul and funk are the live-music staples in the downstairs section of the Blue Nile. Things get pretty sweaty and sensual in the upstairs balcony room, with its dedicated dance floor, as the night goes on. (📞504-948-2583; www.bluenilelive.com; 532 Frenchmen St; cover $10-20; ⏰8pm-late Mon-Wed, 7pm-4am Thu-Sat, 5:30pm-1am Sun)

Maison

LIVE MUSIC

40 ⭐ MAP P60, A3

With three stages, a kitchen and a decent bar, Maison is one of the more varied performance spaces on Frenchmen St. On any given night you may be hearing Latin rumba in one hour, indie rock in another and brass to round out the evening. (📞504-371-5543; www.maisonfrenchmen.com; 508 Frenchmen St; cover $5-10; ⏰4pm-2am Mon-Thu, 1pm-4am Fri & Sat, 10am-2am Sun)

Explore ✦
CBD & Warehouse District

The Central Business District (CBD) and Warehouse District have long been a membrane between down-river Creole faubourgs (neighborhoods) like the French Quarter and the large leafy lots of the Garden District and Uptown. This is an area that has always been in search of an identity, in a city with a distinct sense of place. These days it asserts itself via cultural institutions and convention center infrastructure.

Along Canal St, you'll find theaters like the Saenger, two Audubon museums and a posh mall. Heading south, once you pass Poydras St you're in the Warehouse District. Fulton St runs by old warehouse exteriors, Julia St is the home of many of the city's most expensive art galleries, and around Camp St and St Joseph St, you'll find a cluster of some of the city's most important museums.

Getting There & Around

🚕 A cab from Louis Armstrong Airport costs $36 for one or two people.

🚃🚌 Amtrak and Greyhound (bus) stations, also known as the Union Passenger Terminal, border Loyola Ave.

🚋 St Charles, Canal, Riverfront and Rampart St streetcars connect the area to the French Quarter and other neighborhoods.

Neighborhood Map on p78

Central Business District at dusk SEAN PAVONE/SHUTTERSTOCK ©

Top Sight 📷
National WWII Museum

The National WWII Museum drops you into the action. Wall-sized photographs capture the confusion of D-Day. A stroll through the snowy woods of Ardennes feels eerily cold. Exhibits like these make this grand facility engaging; artifacts, battles and war strategies are humanized through personal recollections and heat-of-the-action displays.

◉ MAP P78, D7

📞 504-528-1944

www.nationalww2mu-seum.org

945 Magazine St

adult/senior/child $27/23.50/17.50, plus 1/2 films $5/10

🕘 9am-5pm

Welcome to World War II

This extensive museum presents a fairly thorough analysis of the most significant war in history. The exhibits, which are displayed across multiple grand pavilions, are enormous and immersive. The experience is designed to be both personal and awe-inducing, but with that said, the museum focuses so intently on providing the American perspective, it sometimes underplays the narrative of other Allied nations.

Campaigns of Courage

The Campaigns of Courage Pavilion spotlights the European and Pacific theaters. Inside, the Road to Berlin galleries cover European battlefronts. A reconstructed Quonset hut – with a bombed-out roof – brings the air war powerfully close. The Road to Tokyo galleries highlight the Pacific theater, with visitors treading a route that begins in the days after Pearl Harbor and ends with the unconditional Japanese surrender.

Other Exhibits

Beyond all Boundaries takes a 4D look at America's involvement in the war on a 120ft-wide screen. Get ready for rumbling seats and a dusting of snowflakes! *Final Mission* is a similar experience that places visitors in the USS submarine *Tang*.

Why New Orleans

How did this fascinating place land in New Orleans, not Washington, DC? The reconstructed LCVP or 'Higgins boat,' on display in the Louisiana Pavilion, provides the link. Originally designed by local entrepreneur Andrew Jackson Higgins for commercial use on Louisiana's bayous, these flat-bottomed amphibious landing craft moved tens of thousands of soldiers onto Normandy's beaches during the D-Day invasion on June 6, 1944.

★ **Top Tips**

o Fair warning: weekends can get packed here. A weekday visit can be a more manageable experience.

o Visitors can personalize their explorations by registering for a dog tag, which connects them with the same WWII participant at various exhibits.

o The on site **BB's Stage Door Canteen** presents weekly 1940s-era live entertainment.

✗ **Take a Break**

Grab a bite in the museum's on-site restaurant, **American Sector** (☑ 504-528-1940; www. american-sector.com; 945 Magazine St; lunch $10-14, dinner $14-28; ⊙ 11am-7pm Sun-Thu, to 8pm Fri & Sat).

Grab an amazing sandwich at Cochon Butcher (p84).

Top Sight 📷
Ogden Museum of Southern Art

Although the Ogden Museum sits just a few steps away from the pedestal that once enshrined Robert E Lee, this vibrant collection of Southern art is not stuck in the past. It's one of the most engaging museums in New Orleans, managing to be beautiful, educational and unpretentious all at once.

👁 **MAP P78, C7**

📞 504-539-9650

www.ogdenmuseum.org

925 Camp St

adult/child 5-17yr
$13.50/6.75

🕙10am-5pm Fri-Wed, to
8pm Thu

Main Exhibition

The Ogden is affiliated with the Smithsonian Institute in Washington, DC, giving it access to that bottomless collection. The glass-and-stone **Stephen Goldring Hall**, with its soaring atrium, provides an inspiring welcome to the grounds. On the top floor, you'll find an excellent collection of Southern folk art sourced from across the region. The building, which opened in 2003, is home to the museum's 20th- and 21st-century exhibitions as well as the **Museum Store** and its **Center for Southern Craft & Design**. 'Floating' stairs connect the different floors.

The Museum Store

The Ogden boasts a very fine museum store, stuffed with prints, crafts and books that explore the theme of regional art. Start with graphite pencils, move on to locally penned coffee table books on New Orleans art and music, then finish with a handcrafted sycamore bowl.

Ogden Origins

The collection got its start more than 30 years ago when Roger Ogden and his father began purchasing art as gifts for Roger's mother. Ogden soon became a passionate collector and by the 1990s the New Orleans entrepreneur had assembled one of the finest collections of Southern art anywhere. Today his namesake museum and its galleries hold pieces that range from impressionist landscapes and outsider folk art to contemporary installation work.

★ **Top Tips**

o Ogden after Hours on Thursdays lets you listen to music and sip wine among masterpieces.

o Start at the top floor and work your way down to get the most out of the experience (and make it easier on your legs).

✄ **Take a Break**

Grab a beautiful tropical meal at Carmo (p83).

For excellent cheese and sandwiches, head to St James (p83).

Walking Tour 🥾

The Past is the Present is the Future

In the Warehouse District, the city's well-worn historical identity rubs shoulders with contemporary cool. On this little tour you'll take in elements of New Orleans ranging from its deep past to its envisioned new horizons – at the least, horizons envisaged by those who think the city can be contemporary and hip while retaining her centuries-old sense of place.

Walk Facts
Start Seaworthy
End Compère Lapin
Length 1.2 miles; 2 hours

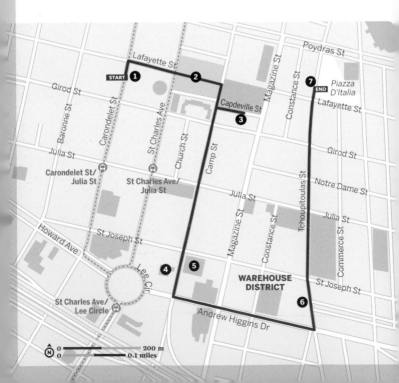

❶ The Ace Hotel & Seaworthy

The drop-dead gorgeous Ace Hotel chain can sometimes feel painfully hip and grounded in global hipster aesthetic. Yet the on-site restaurant, Seaworthy (p82), goes to great pains to specifically draw from the bounty of local waters. We respect that, and the oyster bar, which you should try. Oysters = good walking fuel.

❷ Lafayette Square

As millennial fresh as the Ace may be, walk just a few blocks east (or in local parlance, towards the river) and you're in Lafayette Sq, the second-oldest park in the city, named for a Revolutionary War hero and studded with statues of his contemporaries.

❸ Capdeville

Running off Lafayette Sq is Capdeville St, which is the location of a **bar** (☑504-371-5161; www.capdevillenola.com; 520 Capdeville St; ⏰11am-2:30pm & 5-11pm Mon-Thu, 11am-midnight Fri, from 4pm Sat) of the same name. Both the street and the bar are frequented by digital-age employees who work within the burgeoning tech sector of New Orleans, nicknamed 'Silicon Bayou'.

❹ Southern Art

Within the Ogden Museum of Southern Art (p74), you'll find both old-school and modern interpretations of the American South: its landscapes, its peoples, its hopes and its visions.

❺ Contemporary Arts Center

Across the street from the Ogden is the CAC (p80), where the cutting edge of contemporary art is exhibited. In contrast to the solid brick, 19th- and early 20th century architecture of the nearby warehouses, the flash CAC practically screams its modernity to the city.

❻ Preservation Resource Center

At the Preservation Resource Center (p81), dedicated to preserving the city's historical character, you can learn all about the deep histories of each of New Orleans' neighborhoods.

❼ Compère Lapin

Finish this walk at Compère Lapin (p82), a restaurant that fuses the food and folkways of both the Caribbean and Creole Louisiana with a distinctly 21st-century approach to food presentation and sourcing. Bonus: the cocktails are delicious.

FRENCH QUARTER

CENTRAL BUSINESS DISTRICT

Mississippi River

Moonwalk

Woldenberg Park

Aquarium of the Americas

Harrah's Casino

Hyatt Regency

New Orleans Public Library

Toulouse St
St Peter St
Wilkinson St
Chartres St
Royal St
Toulouse St
St Louis St
Conti St
Dauphine St
Burgundy St
Bourbon St
Iberville St
Exchange Pl
Bienville St
Chartres St
Royal St
Decatur St
Clinton St
Union St
N Front St
N Peters St
Clay St
Bienville St
Canal St
Camp St
Chartres St
Common St
St Charles Ave/
Union St
Gravier St
Perdido St
St Charles Ave/
Poydras St
Canal St/
Peters St
Canal St
Bourbon St
Carondelet St
St Charles Ave/
Common St
Baronne St
Roosevelt Way
Canal St
Rampart St
Crozat St
Basin St
Trente St
Canal St/
Basin St
Elk Pl
Tulane Ave
S Liberty St
S Villere St
Grauier St
La Salle St
S Villere St
Perdido St
Poydras St
Poydras St
O'Keefe Ave
Penn St
Carondelet St/
Poydras St
Canal St/
Rampart St
S Rampart St
Cleveland St
Marais St
Robertson St
S Villere St
Tulane Ave

Insectarium
Shops at Canal Place
S Peters St
Tchoupitoulas St
Magazine St
Natchez St
Camp St/
Poydras St

Canal St Wharf
Canal Street Ferry

• 1
2
13 ✕
29
17 ✕
23
16 ✕
28
22 ✕
20 ✕

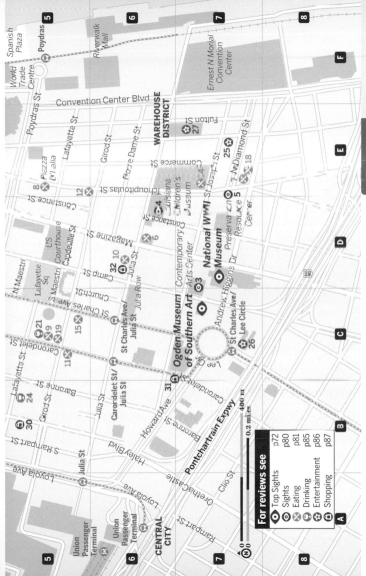

CBD & Warehouse District

Spanish Plaza

World Trade Centre

Poydras

Poydras St

Convention Center Blvd

Lafayette St

Girod St

Notre Dame St

WAREHOUSE DISTRICT

Riverwalk Mall

Ernest N Morial Convention Center

Pizza 8 ⊗ d'Italia

Constance St

Tchoupitoulas St

Commerce St

12 ⊗

Fulton St

27 ⊗

N Diamond St

Louisiana Children's Museum

Magazine St

4 ⊗

Constance St

25 ⊗

St Joseph St

7 ⊗

N Peters St

18 ⊗

6 ⊗

US Courthouse

Capdeville St

Camp St

Julia St

32 ⊗ 10

Church St

National WWII Museum

Preservation Resource Center

5

N Maestri

Lafayette Sq

S Maestri

St Charles Ave/ Julia St

Julia Row

3 ⊙

Ogden Museum of Southern Art

Contemporary Arts Center

Andrew Higgins Dr

15 ⊗

Carondelet St

21 ⊕ 9 ⊗ 19

Lee Circle

St Charles Ave/ Lee Circle

26 ✪

Lafayette St

11 ⊗

Baronne St

Carondelet St/ Julia St

S Charles Ave

Girod St

24

30

S Rampart St

Julia St

Haley Blvd

Howard Ave

31

Carondelet St

Baronne St

Pontchartrain Expwy

Loyola Ave

Union Passenger Terminal

Union Passenger Terminal

CENTRAL CITY

Rampart St

Clio St

Orethacastle

Carondelet St

0 400 m
0 0.2 miles

Sights

Aquarium of the Americas
AQUARIUM

1 ◎ MAP P78, F4

The immense Aquarium of the Americas is loosely regional, with exhibits delving beneath the surface of the Mississippi River, Gulf of Mexico, Caribbean Sea and far-off Amazon rain forest. The impressive Great Maya Reef lures visitors into a 30ft-long clear tunnel running through a 'submerged' Mayan city, now home to exotic fish. Upstairs, the penguin colony, the sea-horse gallery, a bird jungle and a tank for otters are perennially popular. In the Mississippi River Gallery, look for the white alligator. (☏504-581-4629; www.auduboninstitute.org; 1 Canal St; adult/senior/child $30/25/22; ◷10am-5pm Tue-Sun; 👪)

Insectarium
ZOO

2 ◎ MAP P78, E3

We'll be honest: if you're not a fan of bugs and creepy-crawlies, you may be happier elsewhere, because at this lively museum, you'll do more than stare at insects: you'll listen to them, touch them and, if you dare, even taste them. It's a multisensory adventure that's especially fun for kids. Our favorite exhibit? The Japanese-inspired Butterfly Garden, a tranquil slice of Zen pathways where clouds of butterflies hover over pools of koi fish. (☏504-581-4629; https://audubonnatureinstitute.org/insectarium; 423 Canal St, US Custom House; adult/child/senior $23/18/20; ◷10am-4:30pm Tue-Sun; 👪)

Contemporary Arts Center
ARTS CENTER

3 ◎ MAP P78, D7

From the outside, the CAC is pretty unassuming. But once inside, with the grand modernist entrance, an airy, spacious vault with soaring ceilings and conceptual metal and wooden accents, it's impressive. The best reason to visit? A good crop of rotating exhibitions by local as well as international artists, plus a packed events calendar that includes plays, skits, dance and concerts. (CAC; ☏504-528-3805; www.cacno.org; 900 Camp St; adult/student/child $10/$8/free; ◷11am-5pm Wed-Mon)

Louisiana Children's Museum
MUSEUM

4 ◎ MAP P78, D6

This educational museum is like a high-tech kindergarten where the wee ones can play in interactive bliss till nap time. Lots of corporate sponsorship equals lots of hands-on exhibits. The Little Port of New Orleans gallery spotlights the five types of ships found in the local port. Kids can play in a galley kitchen or they can load cargo. Elsewhere, kids can check out optical illusions, shop in a pretend grocery store or frolic in a paper-and-cardboard story forest. (☏504-523-1357; www.lcm.org; 420 Julia St; $10; ◷9:30am-4:30pm Tue-Sat, noon-4:30pm Sun; 👪)

Preservation Resource Center HISTORIC BUILDING

5 ◎ MAP P78, E7

If you're interested in the architecture of New Orleans or a self-guided walking tour, then start here. The welcoming Preservation Resource Center, located inside the 1853 Leeds-Davis building, offers free pamphlets with walking-tour maps for virtually every part of town. The helpful staff shares information about everything from cycling routes to renovating a historic home. Check the website for details about the Shotgun House tour in March and the popular Holiday Home tour in December. (☑504-581 7032; www.prcno.org; 923 Tchoupitoulas St; admission free; ⊙9am-5pm Mon-Fri)

Eating

Peche Seafood Grill SEAFOOD $$

6 ✖ MAP P78, D6

Coastal seafood dishes are prepared simply here, but unexpected flourishes – whether from salt, spices or magic – sear the deliciousness onto your taste buds. The vibe is convivial, with a happy crowd savoring among the exposed-brick walls and wooden beams. A large whole fish, made for sharing, is a signature preparation, but we recommend starting with something from the raw bar. (☑504-522-1744; www.pecherestaurant.com; 800 Magazine St; small plates $9-14, mains $14-27; ⊙11am-10pm Sun-Thu, to 11pm Fri & Sat)

Insectarium

MELINA MARA/THE WASHINGTON POST VIA GETTY IMAGES ©

Cochon Butcher (p84)

Cochon

CAJUN $$

7  MAP P78, E7

The phrase 'everything but the squeal' springs to mind at Cochon, regularly named one of New Orleans' best restaurants. Donald Link pays homage to his Cajun culinary roots and the menu revels in most parts of the pig, including pork cheeks with sweet potato gratin and fried boudin (spicy sausage). (504-588-2123; www.cochonrestaurant.com; 930 Tchoupitoulas St; small plates $8-14, mains $19-32; 11am-10pm Mon-Thu, to 11pm Fri & Sat)

Compère Lapin

CARIBBEAN $$

8 MAP P78, E5

Chef Nina Compton became a household name via the TV show *Top Chef,* but her New Orleans restaurant is anything but a celebrity flash in the pan. This is wonderful cuisine that sits at the intersection of the Caribbean and Louisiana Creole taste universes, serving curry goat and sweet potato gnocchi and jerk drum fish. (504-599-2119; http://comperelapin.com; 535 Tchoupitoulas St; lunch $14-28, dinner $26-31; dinner 5:30-10pm daily, lunch 11:30am-2:30pm Mon-Fri, brunch 10:30am-2pm Sat & Sun;)

Seaworthy

SEAFOOD $$

9 MAP P78, C5

Many new restaurants in New Orleans have not lived up to the city's intimidating culinary legacy. Seaworthy is not such a place. They serve, simply, seafood – gorgeously fresh, brilliantly executed seafood, from yellowfin and sea bass to redfish in chili butter to one of the finest raw oyster selections in the city. (☎504-930-3071; www.seaworthynola.com; 630 Carondelet St; mains $17-30; ☺brunch 11am-3pm Sat & Sun, dinner 5-11pm daily, bar menu 11pm-1am daily)

Carmo VEGETARIAN $

10 MAP P78, D6

Carmo isn't just an alternative to the fatty, carnivorous New Orleans menu – it's an excellent restaurant by any gastronomic measuring stick. Both the aesthetic and the food speak to deep tropical influences, from Southeast Asia to South America. Dishes range from pescatarian to full vegan; try Peruvian style sashimi or Burmese tea leaf salad and walk away happy. (☎504-875-4132; www.cafecarmo.com; 527 Julia St; lunch $9-12, dinner $9-15; ☺11am-3pm Mon, to 10pm Tue & Wed, to 11pm Thu-Sat; 🖉)

Drip Affogato ICE CREAM $

11 MAP P78, C5

Drip serves all kinds of gelato and espresso, but it truly shines when it combines the two into an affogato – espresso or coffee poured onto ice cream. The result is culinary dynamite. If you've just had a good meal downtown, this is the perfect dessert follow up. (☎504-313-1611; www.dripaffogatobar.com; 703 Carondelet St; affogato $8.25; ☺10am-10pm; 🖐)

St James Cheese Company DELI $

12 MAP P78, E5

When it comes to grabbing a sandwich downtown, we're always torn between this spot and Cochon Butcher (p84). St James does possess an advantage on the actual cheese front – this is partly a cheese shop – and you'd be remiss not to try their simple, perfect ham and brie on a baguette. (☎504-304-1485; https://stjamescheese.com; 641 Tchoupitoulas St; mains $7-14; ☺11am-6pm Mon-Wed, to 8pm Thu & Fri, 9am-8pm Sat)

Restaurant August CREOLE $$$

13 MAP P78, E4

For a little romance, reserve a table at Restaurant August. This converted 19th-century tobacco warehouse, with its flickering candles and warm, soft shades, earns a nod for most aristocratic dining room in New Orleans, but somehow manages to be both intimate and lively. Delicious meals take you to another level of gastronomic perception. (☎504-299-9777; www.restaurantaugust.com; 301 Tchoupitoulas St; lunch $23-38, dinner $34-48, 5-course tasting menu $98, with wine pairings $163; ☺5-10pm daily, 11am-2pm Fri; 🖉)

La Boca STEAK $$$

14 MAP P78, E7

The steakhouse scene in New Orleans has been steadily improving over the last decade, and La

Boca has given the city no small push in the polls. Meticulously sourced beef is cooked and cut Argentine style, from hanger steaks to sweetbreads to sirloin flap. (☎504-525-8205; www.labocasteaks.com; 870 Tchoupitoulas St; mains $38-60; ⏱5:30-10pm Mon-Wed, to midnight Thu-Sat)

Herbsaint
LOUISIANAN $$

15 MAP P78, C5

Herbsaint's duck and andouille (smoked sausage) gumbo might be the best restaurant gumbo in town. The rest of the food ain't too bad either – it's very much modern bistro fare with dibs and dabs of Louisiana influence, courtesy of owner Donald Link. On our last visit, we enjoyed divine cornmeal fried oysters and crispy goat served alongside curried cauliflower. (☎504-524-4114; www.herbsaint.com; 701 St Charles Ave; mains $16-34; ⏱11:30am-10pm Mon-Fri, from 5:30pm Sat)

Domenica
ITALIAN $$

16 MAP P78, C3

With its wooden refectory tables, white lights and soaring ceiling, Domenica feels like a village trattoria gone posh. The 'rustic' pizza pies at this lively spot are loaded with nontraditional but enticing toppings – clams, prosciutto, smoked pork – and are big enough that solo diners might just have a slice or two left over. (☎504-648-6020; www.domenicarestaurant.com; 123 Baronne St; mains $15-34; ⏱11am-11pm; ✎)

Luke
BISTRO $$

17 MAP P78, D4

This spin on a European bistro has an elegantly simple tiled interior and a menu that will make you reconsider the limits of Louisiana-French fusion; the primary muse is the smoky, rich cuisine of Alsace, the French–German border. Yellowfin tuna is rubbed with tasso (spicy cured pork), while an entrecôte ribeye comes doused in a sinfully rich bearnaise. (☎504-378-2840; www.lukeneworleans.com; 333 St Charles Ave; mains $16-35; ⏱7am-11pm)

Cochon Butcher
SANDWICHES $

18 MAP P78, E7

Tucked behind the slightly more formal Cochon, this sandwich and meat shop calls itself a 'swine bar and deli.' We call it one of our favorite sandwich shops in the city, if not the South. From the convivial lunch crowds to the savory sandwiches to the fun-loving cocktails, this welcoming place encapsulates the best of New Orleans. (☎504-588-7675; www.cochonbutcher.com; 930 Tchoupitoulas St; mains $10-14; ⏱10am-10pm Mon-Thu, to 11pm Fri & Sat, to 4pm Sun)

Balise
SOUTHERN US $$

19 MAP P78, C5

Peeling plaster and brick accents ensconce a warm, wooden interior where decadent, yet classically inspired, Southern cuisine rules the roost – try the fried-chicken sandwich, a strip steak with roasted bone marrow or fries smothered in pork-cheek gravy and cheese. (☑504-459-4449; www.balisenola. com; 640 Carondelet St; mains $16-34; ⊙lunch & brunch 11:30am-2pm Fri, to 2:30pm Sat & Sun, dinner 4:30-10pm Sun-Thu, to 11pm Fri & Sat)

Pho Tau Bay   VIETNAMESE $

20 🔵 MAP P78, A2

If you ever have a health emergency around lunchtime, head here – this beloved New Orleans Vietnamese hangout is packed with medical staffers in scrubs on an almost daily basis. They come for delicious mains from *banh mi* (Vietnamese sandwiches) to *bun cha* (char grilled pork and vermicelli) to, of course, pho. (☑504-368-9846; www.photaubayrestaurant. com; 1565 Tulane Ave; mains $6.50-13; ⊙10am-7pm Mon-Fri; 🅿)

Drinking

Alto   ROOFTOP BAR

21 🔵 MAP P78, C5

If you want a good view of the city, or a good view of a bunch of millennials enjoying a good view of the city, head to the Ace Hotel's rooftop bar. There's lush greenery, cold mixed drinks, hot breezes and a general sexy-times vibe – as well as a small menu of bar bites. (☑504-900-1180; www.acehotel.com/neworleans/alto; 600 Carondelet St; ⊙10am-9pm)

Handsome Willy's   BAR

22 🔵 MAP P78, A1

Willy's is one of the oddest bars in New Orleans, a neighborhood-style dive in a patch of empty parking lots that lacks a neighborhood. It's consistently fun – there's a nice outdoor area and DJs frequently spin excellent hip-hop and dance tracks. (☑504-525-0377; 218 S Robertson St; ⊙11am-11pm Mon-Wed, to 1am Thu, to 2am Fri, 4pm-2am Sat, to midnight Sun)

Piscobar   COCKTAIL BAR

23 🔵 MAP P78, C3

One of the more haute and hip options in downtown New Orleans, the downstairs bar at the **Catahoula** (☑504-603-2442; www. catahoulahotel.com; 914 Union St; d $230-480, q $300; 🅿❄🛜) specializes in pisco-based cocktails, in case it wasn't obvious (Pisco, for the uninitiated, is a brandy from Peruvian and Chilean wine regions). You'd think this would make for a one-trick-pony bar, but the cocktails here are diverse and delicious. (☑504-603-2442; www.catahoulahotel.com/piscobar/; 914 Union St; ⊙1-10pm Sun-Thu, to midnight Fri & Sat)

CellarDoor   COCKTAIL BAR

24 🔵 MAP P78, B5

Although the CellarDoor is technically a gastropub, we tend to skip the New Southern food menu and lean into the excellent, extensive cocktail list and historic-chic

The Canal Street Ferry

The **Canal Street Ferry** (Map p78, F4; 504-376-8233; www.norta.com/Maps-Schedules/New-Orleans-Ferry; per person $2; 6am-9:45pm Mon-Thu, to 11:45pm Fri, 10:30am-11:45pm Sat, 10:30am-9:45pm Sun) runs from the foot of Canal St to Algiers Point. It's the easiest way to get out on the Mississippi River and admire New Orleans from the traditional river approach (which smells like mud, poo and petroleum).

On weekdays, the ferry leaves Canal St on the quarter hour and the half hour and returns from Algiers on the hour and half hour. On weekends, the schedule flips, with the ferry leaving Canal St on the hour. On the Algiers side, stretch your legs and learn about Louis Armstrong and other jazz greats on the Jazz Walk of Fame along the levee.

ambiance. Once a brothel, this lovely space now doubles (or triples?) as a bar and miniature art gallery. (504-265-8392; www.cellardoornola.com; 916 Lafayette St; 4-11pm Mon-Thu, 4pm-1am Fri, 5pm-1am Sat)

Entertainment

Howlin' Wolf   LIVE MUSIC

 25   MAP P78, E7

One of New Orleans' better venues for live blues, alt-rock, jazz, comedy and roots music, the Howlin' Wolf draws a lively crowd. The attached 'Den' features smaller acts in a more intimate venue. (504-529-5844; www.thehowlinwolf.com; 907 S Peters St; cover from $5; hours vary)

Circle Bar   LIVE MUSIC

 26   MAP P78, C7

Picture a grand Victorian mansion, all disheveled and punk, and you've caught the essence of this strangely inviting place to drink. Live acts of varying quality – folk, rock and indie – occupy the central space, where a little fireplace and lots of grime speak to the coziness of one of New Orleans' great dives. (504-588-2616; www.circlebarneworleans.com; 1032 St Charles Ave; 4pm-2am)

Republic New Orleans   LIVE MUSIC

 27   MAP P78, E7

Republic showcases some pretty awesome live acts, but on any given night the crowd could range from a bunch of music-obsessed fanatics to some aggro meat-heads coming in from the 'burbs. With that said, the curation of acts has gotten better and better over the years and the sight lines to the small stage are awesome. (504-528-8282;

www.republicnola.com; 828 S Peters
St; cover $10-50; ⏱hours vary)

Orpheum Theater
PERFORMING ARTS

28 ⭐ MAP P78, C2

Built back in 1918, this Beaux Arts
beauty is a grand-dame theater
that has undergone many incarna-
tions – vaudeville stage, movie
house etc – and is now the home
of the Louisiana Philharmonic Or-
chestra. It also hosts a ton of gigs
and performances – it's a popular
spot for visiting artists, who love
the restored glory of this venue.
(📞504-274-4870; https://orpheum-
nola.com; 129 Roosevelt Way)

Shopping

Meyer the Hatter
FASHION & ACCESSORIES

29 🔒 MAP P78, D3

This cluttered shop a half-block
from Canal St has a truly astound-
ing inventory of world-class hats.
Biltmore, Dobbs and Stetson
are just a few of the milliners
represented. Fur felts dominate
in fall and winter, and flimsy
straw hats take over in spring and
summer. The selection of lids for
the ladies isn't as deep. (📞504-
525-1048; www.meyerthehatter.com;
120 St Charles Ave; ⏱10am-5:45pm
Mon-Sat)

Stonefree
CLOTHING

30 🔒 MAP P78, B5

This hip little boutique feels
plucked out of Magazine St – or
Brooklyn for that matter. Fun
spangly dresses and styles that
comfortably juke between vintage
and modern are all present and
accounted for. (📞504-304-5485;
http://shopstonefree.com; 611 O'Keefe
Ave; ⏱10am-8pm Mon-Sat, to 6pm
Sun)

Keife and Co
FOOD & DRINKS

31 🔒 MAP P78, C6

This chic little gastronomic
boutique is packed with fancy
charcuterie, teas, caviar, condi-
ments, wines, spirits and all the
other ingredients of a fairly expensive, if extremely, enjoyable picnic.
(📞504-523-7272; www.keifeandco.
com; 801 Howard Ave; ⏱10am-8pm
Tue-Sat)

Ariodante
ARTS & CRAFTS

32 🔒 MAP P78, D6

This small but well-stocked gallery
sells jewelry, glass works, ceramics
and fine art by local and regional
artists. It's a fun place to browse.
(📞504-524-3233; www.ariodantegal-
lery.com; 535 Julia St; ⏱9:30am-4pm
Mon-Sat, to 1:30pm Sun)

Explore ◈

Garden, Lower Garden & Central City

As one proceeds south along the curve of the Mississippi River, the streets become tree lined and the houses considerably grander. The Garden District exudes Old Southern excess with its historic mansions, lush greenery, chichi bistros and upscale boutiques. On your first morning, soak up the mixture of tropical, fecund beauty and white-columned, old-money elegance on a walking tour, where stately homes and colorful gardens shimmer beside sidewalks bursting with roots.

Between the CBD and the Garden District, the Lower Garden District is somewhat like the Garden District but not quite as posh. Here the houses are pleasant, not palatial. There's a studenty vibe, and plenty of bars and restaurants for those with university-stunted wallets and university-sized appetites for fun.

Getting There & Around

🚌 Bus 11 runs along Magazine St from Canal St to Audubon Park.

🚋 The St Charles Avenue Streetcar route travels through the CBD, the Garden District and Uptown.

Neighborhood Map on p94

Top Sight 📷
Lafayette Cemetery No 1

A thick wall surrounds a battalion of gray crypts at this moody place, a tiny bastion of history, tragedy and Southern Gothic charm in the heart of the Garden District. Of all the cemeteries in New Orleans, Lafayette exudes the strongest sense of subtropical Southern Gothic.

👁 **MAP P94, B3**

📞 504-658-3781

Washington Ave, at Prytania St

admission free

🕐 7am-3pm

A Mournful Layout

The cemetery is divided by two intersecting footpaths that form a cross. Look out for the structures built by fraternal organizations such as the Jefferson Fire Company No 22, which took care of its members and their families in large shared crypts. The spell here is admittedly broken the moment a black-and-white-clad waiter strides past the cemetery's grated gates, hurrying to his shift at the neighboring Commander's Palace restaurant. He's a vivid reminder that time marches on.

Types of Tombs

The stark contrast of moldering crypts and gentle decay with the forceful fertility of the fecund greenery is incredibly jarring. Some of the wealthier family tombs were built of marble, with elaborate detail rivaling the finest architecture in the district, but most tombs were constructed simply of inexpensive plastered brick. You'll notice many German and Irish names on the above-ground graves, evidence of both those communities' arrival to America as immigrants.

History of a Necropolis

The cemetery was built in 1833 and filled to capacity within decades of its opening, before the surrounding neighborhood reached its greatest affluence. Indeed, not far from the entrance is a tomb containing the remains of an entire family that died of yellow fever. By 1872 the prestigious Metairie Cemetery in Mid-City had opened and its opulent grounds appealed to those with truly extravagant and flamboyant tastes. In July 1995, author Anne Rice staged her own funeral here. She hired a horse-drawn hearse and a brass band to play dirges, and wore an antique wedding dress as she laid down in a coffin. The event coincided with the release of one of Rice's novels.

★ Top Tips

o During the summer months, don't underestimate how big the cemetery is, and how hot the area can be. Take some water with you.

o Keep an eye out for the various society crypts that hold deceased members of community organizations, ranging from firemen to orphans.

✕ Take a Break

Well, the legendary Creole restaurant Commander's Palace (p97) is just across the street...

You could also wander up to the old-school **Verret's Lounge** (☏ 504-895-9640; 1738 Washington Ave; ◷3pm-3am Sun-Thu, to 4am Fri & Sat) for a quick drink.

Walking Tour 🥾

Green, Green New Orleans

Soak up the 'green' of New Orleans from the historic, magnolia-shaded streets of the Garden District to the Emerald Isle heritage of the Irish Channel.

Walk Facts

Start The Rink

Finish Tracey's

Length 1 mile; two to three hours

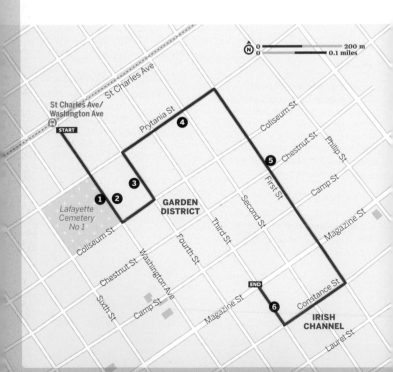

❶ The Rink & Around

From the CBD, take the St Charles Avenue Streetcar to Washington Ave. Walk one block south to the Rink, an 1880s skating rink turned 21st-century mini-mall. Lafayette Cemetery No 1 (p90), one of the city's oldest cemeteries, stands across Prytania St.

❷ Commander's Palace

Just across the street from the cemetery is the dapper Commander's Palace (p97), the elegant crown jewel of the Brennan restaurant empire. Pop in for a 25¢ martini at lunchtime, but remember – no shorts allowed.

❸ Fourth Street

Around the corner at 1448 Fourth St is **Colonel Robert Short's House**, designed by architect Henry Howard. Once the home of a Confederate officer, it's an exemplary double-gallery home with fine cast-iron details, including a cast iron cornstalk fence.

❹ Prytania St & First St

Continue to the **Women's Guild of the New Orleans Opera Association** at 2504 Prytania, a Greek Revival home designed by William Freret in the late 1850s. Turn right onto First St, where you'll find **Joseph Carroll House** at No 1315, a beautiful center-hall house with double galleries laced with cast iron.

❺ Anne Rice's Residence

The grand home at **1239 First St** is the former residence of author Anne Rice. The spinner of vampire tales lived in the 1857 home for many years, and regularly invited fans to tour inside. Which, by the way, is beautiful but disappointingly free of Tom Cruise in a frilly jacket. It's no longer open to the public.

❻ Entering the Irish Channel

Head down First St, turn right into Constance and wander along until you come to Parasol's (p98) on the corner of Third St and **Tracey's** (☎504-897-5413; www.traceysnola.com; 2604 Magazine St; mains $9-15; ⏱11am-10pm Sun-Thu, to midnight Fri & Sat, bar 11am-late) on the corner of Third and Magazine Sts. These are two quintessential New Orleans neighborhood bars with dueling roast beef po'boy sandwiches. Dig in.

Garden, Lower Garden & Central City

Greater New Orleans Bridge (toll)

Port of New Orleans Pl

Blaine Kern's Mardi Gras World **5**

Mississippi River

500 m
0.25 miles

Pontchartrain Expwy

CENTRAL CITY

Southern Food & Beverage **2**

Ashé Cultural Arts Center

GARDEN DISTRICT

IRISH CHANNEL

Lafayette Cemetery No 1

Van McMurray Playground

Lafayette Cemetery No 2

Sights

Coliseum Square
PARK

1 ⊙ MAP P94, D2

Much of the Lower Garden District was designed as a settlement zone for those Americans who began arriving in New Orleans after the Louisiana Purchase. Coliseum Square was envisaged as a sort of triangular village green for those residents and, to be fair, the space still serves as a center of gravity and recreational area for locals looking for fresh air. The park does attract the occasional shady hanger-on come nightfall. (1708 Coliseum St; ⊙24hr)

Southern Food & Beverage Museum
MUSEUM

2 ⊙ MAP P94, C1

You don't have to be a gourmet or mixologist to enjoy this made-from-scratch museum, which celebrates Southern cooking and cocktails with exhibits – some fascinating, others less so – sourced from every state south of the Mason-Dixon line. The well-stocked **Museum of the American Cocktail** displays old elixir bottles, cocktail-making tools, tiki glasses and old pictures of impressively mustachioed bartenders. Check the website for details about cooking classes in the demo kitchen. (☑504-569-0405; www.natfab.org/ southern-food-and-beverage; 1504 Oretha Castle Haley Blvd; adult/child under 12yr $10.50/free; ⊙11am-5:30pm Wed-Mon)

Irish Channel
AREA

3 ⊙ MAP P94, C4

The name Irish Channel is a bit of a misnomer. Although this historic neighborhood, which borders the Garden Districts, was settled by poor Irish immigrants fleeing the 1840s potato famine, many German and African American residents coexisted here in a multicultural gumbo. This is a rapidly gentrifying cluster of shotgun houses, and in general it's pleasant for ambling, although you should exercise caution at night.

Ashé Cultural Arts Center
ARTS CENTER

4 ⊙ MAP P94, C1

An important anchor for the local African American community, Ashé (from a Yoruba word that could loosely be translated as 'Amen') regularly showcases performances, art and photography exhibitions, movie screenings and lectures with an African, African American or Caribbean focus, and beyond. Check the online calendar for upcoming events. (☑504-603-6394; www.ashecac.org; 1712 Oretha Castle Haley Blvd; ⊙10am-6pm Mon-Sat)

Blaine Kern's Mardi Gras World
MUSEUM

5 ⊙ MAP P94, F2

We dare say Mardi Gras World is one of the happiest places in New Orleans by day – but at night it must turn into a terrifying

The American Sector

Following the Louisiana Purchase in 1803, Americans began moving to New Orleans. Shunned by the Creole inhabitants, they settled on the other side of Canal St, building their plantations upriver from the French Quarter. These upriver communities were essentially suburbs, but trade led to wealth and expansion. Land was parceled out of plantations; these 'garden'-sized lots formed the Garden District. In a display of one-upmanship aimed at the Creoles, as well as a homage to the founders of democracy, many built homes in Greek Revival style, fronted by columns and accented by colonnaded galleries.

fun-house. It's all those *faces*: the dragons, clowns, kings and fairies, leering and dead-eyed. That said, we love touring Mardi Gras World – the studio-warehouse of Blaine Kern (Mr Mardi Gras) and family, who have been making jaw-dropping parade floats since 1947. Tours last about 90 minutes, and are given by a crew of knowledgeable, personable docents. (☏504-475-2057; www.mardigrasworld.com; 1380 Port of New Orleans Pl; adult/senior/child 2-11yr $22/17/14; ☺tours 9am-5:30pm, last tour 4pm; ☒🚹)

Eating

Surrey's Juice Bar
AMERICAN $

6 ✖ MAP P94, D2

Surrey's makes a simple bacon-and-egg sandwich taste – and look – like the most delicious breakfast you've ever been served. And you know what? It probably *is* the best. Boudin biscuits; eggs scrambled with salmon; biscuits swimming in salty sausage gravy; and a shrimp, grits and bacon dish that should be illegal. And the juice, as you might guess, is blessedly fresh.

Surrey's has an Uptown branch with the same menu and hours at 4807 Magazine St. (☏504-524-3828; www.surreysnola.com; 1418 Magazine St; mains $6.50-13; ☺8am-3pm; 🚹)

Stein's Deli
DELI $

7 ✖ MAP P94, D3

You may get a no-nonsense 'what?' when you step up to the counter, but it's just part of the schtick at this scruffy deli. For quality sandwiches, cheese and cold cuts, this is as good as the city gets. Owner Dan Stein is fanatical about keeping his deli stocked with great Italian and Jewish meats and cheeses, and fine boutique beers. (☏504-527-0771; www.steinsdeli.net; 2207 Magazine St; sandwiches $7-13; ☺7am-7pm Tue-Fri, 9am-5pm Sat & Sun)

Commander's Palace

CREOLE $$$

8 MAP P94, C3

Commander's Palace is a dapper host, a seer-suckered bon vivant who wows with white-linen dining rooms, decadent dishes and attentive Southern hospitality. The nouveau Creole menu shifts, and can run from crispy oysters with brie cauliflower fondue to pecan crusted gulf fish. The dress code adds to the charm: no shorts or T-shirts, and jackets preferred at dinner. It's a *very* nice place – and lots of fun.

Owner Ella Brennan takes pride in her ability to promote her chefs to stardom; Paul Prudhomme and Emeril Lagasse are among her alumni. And take note that some of that stiff-upper-lip formality is put on; the lunch special, after all, is the 25¢ martini. Reservations are required. (📞504-899-8221; www.commanderspalace.com; 1403 Washington Ave; dinner mains $32-43; ⏲11:30am-1pm & 6:30-10:30pm Mon-Fri, from 11am Sat, from 10am Sun)

Coquette

FRENCH $$

9 MAP P94, C4

Coquette mixes wine-bar ambience with friendly service and a bit of white linen; the result is a candlelit place where you don't feel bad getting tipsy. Explore beyond the respectable wine menu, though – there's some great Louisiana-sourced food here, often with an innovative global spin. Choices may include charred

Commander's Palace

CHARLES O. CECIL/ALAMY STOCK PHOTO ®

MARIANNA DAY MASSEY/ZUMA PRESS ©

Coquette (p97)

and kohlrabi, or speckled trout with shrimp and sausage dressing. (📞504-265-0421; www.coquette-nola.com; 2800 Magazine St; brunch mains $13-23, dinner mains $20-30; 🕙5:30-10pm Mon-Fri, 10:30am-2pm & 5:30-10pm Sat & Sun)

Poke Loa   HAWAIIAN $

10 ✖ MAP P94, B4

A welcome and popular addition to the New Orleans dining firmament, Poke Loa brings Hawaiian-style *poke* bowls (raw fish mixed with vegetables, spices, sauces and other bits of goodness) to Magazine St. There are over 15 toppings and tons of protein and green options to round out your bowl, but the end result is invariably tasty. (📞504-309-9993; www.eatpokeloa.com; 3341 Magazine St; mains $11.50-15; 🕙11am-9pm; 🍴)

Parasol's   SANDWICHES $

11 ✖ MAP P94, C4

Parasol's isn't just in the Irish Channel neighborhood; it sort of *is* the Irish Channel, serving as community center, nexus of gossip and watering hole. It's first and foremost a bar, but you can order some of the best po'boy sandwiches in New Orleans from the seating area in the back. You won't regret it – that big ol' roast beef is a messy, juice-filled conduit of deliciousness. (📞504-302-1533; 2533 Constance St; po'boys $7-16; 🕙11am-9pm)

Dryades Public Market

MARKET $

12 MAP P94, C1

This enormous market is stocked with fresh groceries representing a good range of local vendors, and there are several hot-food bars – the menu varies, but it's invariably good (and good value). On some days we've had great oysters and fried chicken here, on others, excellent teriyaki. Grab some groceries for a picnic too. (504-644-4841; http://dryadespublicmarket.com; 1307 Oretha Castle Haley Blvd, hot plates $8-13; 8am-8pm Mon-Thu, to 9pm Fri & Sat, to 6pm Sun;)

Seed

HEALTH FOOD $

13 MAP P94, D1

Vegetarians and vegans can now nosh with abandon in New Orleans, just like their more carnivorous friends. This spare and boxy addition to the Lower Garden District calls its menu 'garden-based' and whips up delicious salads and sandwiches plus a few heartier mains, such as vegetarian spaghetti and pad Thai. Blended juices and cocktails, all made with fresh juice, add to the fun. (504-302-2599; www.seedyourhealth. com; 1330 Prytania St; mains $7-14; 11am-10pm Mon-Fri, from 10am Sat & Sun;)

Sucré

SWEETS $

14 MAP P94, B4

Willy Wonka's chocolate factory has put away its top-hat and purple suede coat and gone decidedly upscale. Artisanal chocolates, chocolate bars, toffee, marshmallows, gelato and other confections beckon from behind the glass counter. One macaroon will set you back $2 – but you can gain comfort from the fact that Sucré is widely considered the best chocolate in town. (504-520-8311; www.shopsucre.com; 3025 Magazine St; confectionary $2-9, 9am-10pm Sun-Thu, to 11pm Fri & Sat)

Café Reconcile

DINER $

15 MAP P94, C1

Café Reconcile fights the good fight by recruiting and training at-risk youth to work as kitchen and floor staff. The food is simple and, frankly, really good. It's very much of the humble New Orleans school of home cookery: red beans and rice, fried chicken, shrimp Creole and the like, with the spotlight on daily specials. (504-568-1157; http://reconcileneworleans.org; 1631 Oretha Castle Haley Blvd; mains $6-15; 11am-2:30pm Mon-Fri)

Mais Arepas

COLOMBIAN $

16 MAP P94, D1

If the cuisine of the Southern US isn't far enough south for you, head to South America via Mais Arepas. Their specialty is, unsurprisingly, arepas (corn cakes) topped with all sorts of goodies: chicken, avocado and lime juice; fried oysters and salsa; and grilled steak, onions and black beans – to name a few examples. (📞504-523-6247; 1200 Carondelet St; mains $8-20; ⏰11:30am-2:30pm & 6-9:45pm Tue-Sat, 6-9:15pm Sun)

Drinking

Bulldog   BAR

17 🚇 MAP P94, B4

With 40 or so brews on tap and more than 100 by the bottle or can – from Louisiana and Mexico to Italy and points beyond – the Bulldog works hard to keep beer enthusiasts happy. The best place to sink a pint is the courtyard, which gets packed with the young and beautiful almost every evening when the weather is warm. (📞504-891-1516; http://bulldog.draftfreak. com; 3236 Magazine St; ⏰11:30am-2am)

Avenue Pub   PUB

18 🚇 MAP P94, D2

From the street, this scruffy pub looks like a nothing-special neighborhood dive. But with more than 40 beers on tap and another 135-odd in bottles, plus staff with serious dedication to the taste of their drafts, this two-story beer bar is earning national accolades. The upstairs patio is a fine place to watch the world go by. (📞504-586-9243; www.theavenuepub.com; 1732 St Charles Ave; ⏰24hr)

Half Moon   BAR

19 🚇 MAP P94, D3

On an interesting corner, just half a block from Magazine St, the

Half Moon beckons with a cool neighborhood vibe. This dive bar is good for a beer, short-order meal or an evening shooting stick. Look for the sweet neon sign. Hours can be fungible, but they try to keep the kitchen open as long as the bar is open. (📞504-522-0599; www. halfmoongrillnola.com; 1125 St Mary St; ⏰5pm-2am)

Urban South   MICROBREWERY

20 🚇 MAP P94, E3

In an industrial dystopia of warehouses and concrete jungle, you'll find a big, booming beer hall packed with happy folks and, yes, laughing kids. Urban South keeps a couple of things on tap, as it were – over a dozen award-winning beers, and a children's play area with daycare, donated toys and an old arcade game.

They offer free brewery tours at 5pm and 7pm on Friday, 3pm, 5pm and 7pm on Saturday, and 2pm and 4pm on Sunday. (📞504-267-4852; http://urbansouthbrewery.com; 1645 Tchoupitoulas St; ⏰4-9pm Mon-Wed, from noon Thu & Fri, from 11am Sat & Sun; 👶)

Barrel Proof   BAR

21 🚇 MAP P94, E1

Do you like whiskey? We sincerely hope so, because there are almost 300 to pick from here, including smoky, smooth and sublime. The crowd is young professional and dressed to impress, but the ties loosen up as the brown liquor flows. Plenty of other spirits and beers on tap as well. (📞504-299-1888; www.barrelproofnola.com; 1201 Magazine St; 🕑4pm-1am Sun-Thu, to 2am Fri & Sat)

NOLA Brewing BREWERY

22 📍 MAP P94, C4

This cavernous brewery welcomes guests throughout the weekend for a free brewery tour that kicks off with sloshy cups of craft brew and a food truck or two out front. The rest of the week? Stop by the taproom, which has plenty of beers on tap and a roof deck.

As for the brewery tour, it's a high-energy gathering of youngish folks and beer enthusiasts who want to get gently buzzed and hang out in a festival-like setting – and

maybe learn about beer. Beloved originals include the NOLA Blonde and the Hopitoulas. (📞504-301-1117; www.nolabrewing.com; 3001 Tchoupitoulas St; 🕑taproom 11am-11pm, tours 2-3pm Fri, 2-4pm Sat & Sun)

Saint Bar & Lounge BAR

23 📍 MAP P94, D3

The Saint? Of what? How about a great backyard beer garden enclosed in duck blinds and filled with tattooed young professionals, Tulane students, good shots and a fair bit of attitude. It's not the cleanest bar (nickname: the 'aint), but it sure is a fun one (📞504 523 0500; www.thesaint-neworleans.com; 961 St Mary St; 🕑7pm-late)

Funky Monkey (p102)

Shopping

Trashy Diva   CLOTHING

24 🔒 MAP P94, D3

It isn't really as scandalous as the name suggests, except by Victorian standards. Diva's specialty is sassy 1940s- and '50s-style cinched, hourglass dresses and Belle Époque undergarments – lots of corsets, lace and such. The shop also features Kabuki–inspired dresses with embroidered dragons, and retro tops, skirts and shawls reflecting styles plucked from just about every era. (📞504-299-8777; www.trashydiva.com; 2048 Magazine St; 🕑noon-6pm Mon-Fri, from 11am Sat, 1-5pm Sun)

Tchoup Industries   SPORTS & OUTDOORS

25 🔒 MAP P94, D3

A nice bag may turn heads, but it'll drop jaws when your friends notice the canvas siding, vintage metal clasps, or exterior made from a repurposed rice bag. These are all locally sourced materials that go into these immensely popular bags 'for city and swamp', which are often produced from found or sustainable materials. (📞504-872-0726; www.tchoupindustries.com; 1115 St Mary St; 🕑11am-6pm Mon & Tue, Thu-Sat, noon-5pm Sun)

Funky Monkey   VINTAGE

26 🔒 MAP P94, B4

You'll find wigs in every color at Funky Monkey, which sells vintage attire for club-hopping men and women. This fun-house of frippery is also a good spot for Mardi Gras costumes. It's tiny, though, and can get jam-packed with customers. In addition to wigs, look for jeans, jewelry, tops, sunglasses, hats and boots. (📞504-899-5587; www.funkymonkeynola.com; 3127 Magazine St; 🕑11am-6pm Sun-Wed, to 7pm Thu-Sat)

Simon of New Orleans   ARTS & CRAFTS

27 🔒 MAP P94, D3

Local artist Simon Hardeveld has made a name for himself by painting groovy signs that hang like artwork in restaurants all over New Orleans. You'll probably recognize the distinctive stars, dots and sparkles that fill the spaces between letters on colorfully painted signs such as 'Who Died & Made You Elvis?' (📞504-524-8201; 1028 Jackson Ave, Antiques on Jackson; 🕑10am-5pm Mon-Sat)

Disko Obscura   MUSIC

You'd think it was hard enough to be a record shop in this day and age, but along comes Disko Obscura (see 25 🔒 Map p94, D3), a record shop specializing in underground disco, techno, post-punk and synth-based LPs. That's *niche,* but Obscura is also a small recording studio and has a dedicated international clientele. (www.diskoobscura.com; 1113 Saint Mary St; 🕑noon-6pm Fri-Mon)

Aidan Gill for Men

FASHION & ACCESSORIES

28 🔒 MAP P94, D3

Shave and a haircut: 40 bits. Or $40. Apiece. But who's counting at this suave barbershop, where smartly dressed Prohibition–era mobsters would surely have felt comfortable? It's all about looking neat and stylish, in a well-heeled, masculine sort of way. High-end shaving gear and smart men's gifts are sold in front, and the barber shop is in back. (📞504-587-9000; www.aidangillformen.com; 2026 Magazine St; ⏱10am-6pm Mon Wed & Fri, to 7pm Thu, 9am-6pm Sat. noon-6pm Sun)

RHINO

ARTS & CRAFTS

This cool gallery (see **28** 🔒 Map p94, D3) is run by a nonprofit that gathers some of the city's most talented artists and craftspeople. The artists participate in arts education programs aimed at the public, conduct a ton of workshops, and display quirky work in all kinds of major media. A great spot for a local souvenir. (Right Here In New Orleans; 📞504-523-7945; http://rhinocrafts.com; 2028 Magazine St; ⏱10am-5pm Mon-Sat, from noon Sun)

Anton Haardt Gallery

ART

29 🔒 MAP P94, C4

The bold, expressive work of outsider and folk art (produced by those with no formal arts education) is an aesthetic that is in no particularly fit funky, idiosyncratic New Orleans. With work sourced from across the American South, this gallery represents an excellent repository of outsider artistic vision. (📞504-891-9080; www.antonhaardtgallery.com; 2858 Magazine St; ⏱noon-4pm Tue Sat)

Diaspora Boutique

JEWELRY

This boutique (see **4** 🔵 Map p94, C1) sells clothing, jewelry and crafts from across the African diaspora. Some of the prints are stunning, and the shop also has books by small print publishers. (📞504-569-9070; www.facebook.com/ashediasporaboutique; 1712 Oretha Castle Haley Blvd; ⏱9am-5:30pm Mon-Sat)

Explore ◈

Uptown & Riverbend

Uptown is the area where American settlers decided to prove to the original French inhabitants that they could be as tasteful and wealthy as any old-world aristocrat. The views of mansion after mansion on St Charles Ave are worth checking out even if you're not an architecture fan.

Magazine St is one of the coolest strips of restaurants and shopping outlets in town. Eventually the 'U' curves north again along the river's bend into Riverbend, popular with the university crowd.

Check out the Audubon Zoo (p108) in the morning. Magazine St runs past the zoo, so after your visit with the elephants and giraffes, spend the rest of the day exploring the shops and art galleries. Enjoy dinner on Freret St, then catch a band or grab drinks at a local joint such as Tipitina's (p118).

Getting There & Around

🚌 Bus 11 ($1.25) runs along Magazine St from Canal St to Audubon Park.

🚋 The St Charles Avenue Streetcar ($1.25) travels through the CBD, the Garden District and into Uptown/Riverbend.

🚗 Metered car parking ($2 per hour) is required along much of Magazine St between 8am and 7pm Monday through Saturday.

Neighborhood Map on p112

Milton H Latter Memorial Library (p114) CJGK PHOTOGRAPHY/SHUTTERSTOCK ©

Top Sight 📷
St Charles Avenue Streetcar

The clang and swoosh of the St Charles Avenue Streetcar is as essential to Uptown and the Garden District as live oaks and mansions. New Orleanians are justifiably proud of their moving monument, which began life as the nation's second horse-drawn streetcar line, the New Orleans & Carrollton Railroad, in 1835.

◎ MAP P112, E4

📞504-248-3900, TTY 504-827-7832

www.norta.com

per ride $1.25, all-day pass $3

🕓24hr

Quintessential New Orleans Commute

In 1893 the line was among the first streetcar systems in the country to be electrified. Now it is one of the few streetcars in the USA to have survived the automobile era. Millions of passengers utilize the streetcar every day, despite the fact the city's bus service tends to be faster. In many ways, the streetcar is the quintessential vehicle for New Orleans public transportation: slow, pretty and, if not entirely efficient, extremely atmospheric.

Other Lines

Another streetcar line plies Canal St and runs all the way to Greenwood Cemetery; a spur on this line runs along Carrollton Ave to City Park. You can also hop on the Rampart streetcar, which plies Rampart St between the New Orleans **Union Passenger Terminal** (Amtrak 800-872-7245, Greyhound 504-525-6075; 1001 Loyola Ave) and Canal St, where the car continues on Rampart St, skirting the edge of the French Quarter and terminating at Elysian Fields Ave in Faubourg Marigny. Finally, the Riverfront line plies a short route running from Esplanade Ave, at the border of the Quarter and Marigny, and Julia St, in the Warehouse District.

Along the Avenue

It's only slightly hyperbolic to claim St Charles Ave is the most beautiful street in the USA. Once you enter the Garden District and later, Uptown, the entire street is shaded under a tunnel of live oak trees that look like they could have wiped the floor with an orc army in a Tolkien novel (ie they're old, and they're big).

★ Top Tips

o A 'Jazzy Pass' ($3) allows you unlimited rides on the streetcar and buses for a day. Buy from a streetcar operator or use the GoMobile app.

o The streetcar arrives roughly every 20 minutes, 24 hours a day.

✕ Take a Break

Head to **Delachaise** (504-895-0858; www.thedelachaise.com; 3442 St Charles Ave; small plates $8-28, cheese plates $13-28; 5pm-2am Mon Thu, from noon Fri-Sun) for some wine and cheese.

Feeling fancy? Have a mint julep at the Columns (p118).

Top Sight 📷
Audubon Zoo

The zoo is inside Audubon Park, a lovely riverside spot with 1.8 miles of multi-use paved trail unfurling beneath a shady canopy of live oaks. It's a large zoo with numerous different sections, including African, Asian and South American landscapes and fauna, and many of the popular animals from elephants to giraffes that kids love to see.

◎ MAP P112, B5

📞 504-861-2537

6500 Magazine St

adult/child 2-12yr/senior $23/18/20

🕐 10am-5pm Mon-Fri, to 6pm Sat & Sun Sep-Mar, 10am-4pm Tue-Fri, to 5pm Sat & Sun Apr-Aug; 🅿 🚻

Zoo Sections

The zoo's sections have names such as the **Louisiana Swamp**: a Cajun wonderland of bald cypresses and Spanish moss, natural wonders of southern Louisiana bayou country. Bobcats, lynx, alligators, bears and otters are on view here, and you may see a red fox chilling on a log in the swamp scrub.

There's also the **Reptile Encounter**, displaying some of the largest snakes in the world – from the king cobra, which grows to more than 18ft in length, to the green anaconda that reaches 38ft. Other memorable sections include the Mayan-style **Jaguar Jungle** and the **South American Pampas** with its raised walkway.

The Fly

Behind the zoo is the Fly (p111), Audubon Park's waterfront section where people toss Frisbees and chill out, just beyond the levee.

★ Top Tips

o Feeding time is when the animals are most active; check in advance and/or go early.

o The zoo can be incredibly hot in the summer, so go prepared.

o Combo passes are available at the door and online, offering discounts when visiting the zoo, Audubon Aquarium of the Americas and Audubon Butterfly Garden and Insectarium.

o During the summer, part of the zoo becomes a water park for kids.

✕ Take a Break

If an elephant trumpets in your face and you need a drink to calm your nerves, **Monkey Hill Bar** (☎ 504-899-4800; 6100 Magazine St; ☺ 3pm-2am Mon-Thu, to 3am Fri, 1pm-3am Sat, noon-2am Sun) is a few blocks away on Magazine St.

A few blocks further away, also on Magazine, you can grab a nice Italian dinner at Avo (p115).

Walking Tour 🥾

A Day in Audubon Park

Audubon Park is a grand green space, run through with live oak trees, walking and cycling paths and picturesque waterways, all framed by some of the city's grandest residences. Students lounge on the grass under Spanish moss while joggers lope by, dog owners play with their pets, and friends have an outdoor sundowner. Basically, it's an emerald urban idyll.

Walk Facts

Start Audubon Park
End The Fly
Length 4 miles; 3 hours

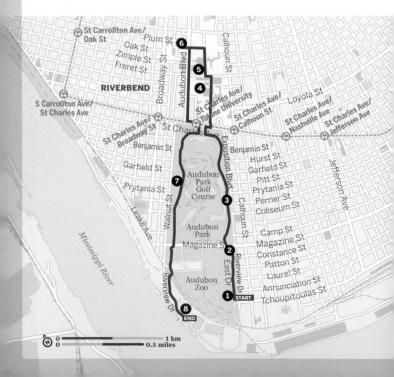

❶ Big Branches

Start your walk on East Dr near the bottom of Audubon Park (p114), where the first landmark is the largest tree in the park: the Etienne de Bore Oak, or Tree of Life. This plant boasts a massive girth of 35ft and a leaf crown more than 160ft wide.

❷ Oak Allee

Oak Allee runs from below Magazine St into the northern half of the park. It's a beautiful, veritable hallway of live oaks, and a favorite spot for dog walkers and those taking early evening lovers' strolls.

❸ Happy Trails

A **nature trail** runs around the entire northern half of the park. At the intersection of the trail and Prytania St, you'll find the muddy waters of Olmstead 'Lake'.

❹ Tulane University

The campus of **Tulane** (☎504-865-5000; www.tulane.edu; 6823 St Charles Ave), a premier Southern university, is a pleasant spot for wandering. The grounds are an attractive tableau of live oaks, red-brick buildings and green quads spread across 110 acres just north of Audubon Park.

❺ A Jazz Journey

Local music fans can often be found at the **Hogan Jazz Archive** (☎504-865-5688; http://jazz.tulane.edu; 6801 Freret St, 3rd fl, Jones Hall, Tulane University, Tulane University; ◷8:30am-5:30pm Mon-Fri), where oral histories comprise the heart of the holdings. This collection of New Orleans jazz artifacts includes sheet music, photographs, journals and recordings. Most of the archive's wealth of material is not exhibited but the helpful staff will retrieve items.

❻ Art Around Audubon

Flanked by stunning Tiffany stained-glass triptychs, the Newcomb Art Museum (p114) is a great spot to soak up art with a local or regional spin. You'll often find Uptowners and students here enjoying the quiet, contemplative atmosphere.

❼ Walnut Mansions

Re-enter Audubon Park from the northwest. As the trail loops around the west end of the park and heads south, it runs adjacent to **Walnut Street** and some of the city's most gorgeous (and expensive) homes.

❽ The Fly

The **Fly** (Riverview Dr, ◷dawn-dusk), an elevated (for New Orleans) area that overlooks the Mississippi River, is the end of your journey. It's one of the most popular picnic spots in the city, and on nice days you'll see families enjoying a beer while children log-roll down the artificial hills.

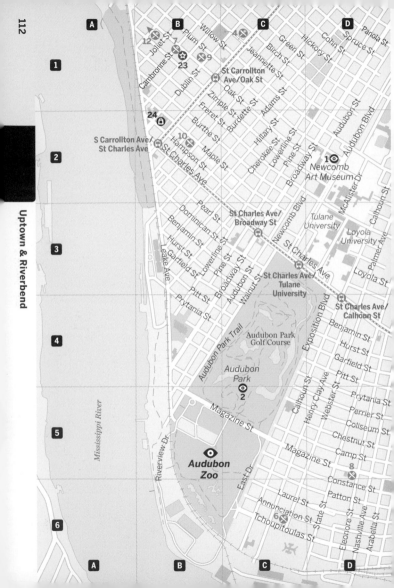

A **B** **C** **D**

Panola St
Spruce St
Cohn St
Hickory St
Green St
Birch St
Jeannette St
Joliet St
Plum St
Willow St
Cambronne St
Dublin St
Oak St
Zimple St
Burdette St
Adams St
Freret St
Burthe St
Maple St
Hillary St
Cherokee St
Lowerline St
Pine St
Broadway St
Audubon St
Audubon Blvd

12
7
9
23
4

St Carrollton
Ave/Oak St

24

S Carrollton Ave/
St Charles Ave

10
Hampson St
St Charles Ave

1
Newcomb
Art Museum

McAlister Dr

Pearl St
Dominican St
Benjamin St
Hurst St
Garfield St
Leake Ave
Lowerline St
Pine St
Broadway St
Pitt St
Prytania St

St Charles Ave/
Broadway St

Newcomb Blvd

Tulane
University

Loyola
University

St Charles Ave

Calhoun St
Palmer Ave
Loyola St

St Charles Ave/
Tulane University

St Charles Ave/
Calhoun St

Exposition Blvd

Benjamin St
Hurst St
Garfield St
Pitt St
Prytania St
Perrier St
Coliseum St
Chestnut St
Camp St

Audubon Park Trail

Audubon Park
Golf Course

Audubon
Park

2

Calhoun St
Henry Clay Ave
Webster St

Mississippi River

Riverview Dr

Magazine St

Audubon
Zoo

East Dr

Magazine St

8

Constance St
Patton St
Laurel St
Annunciation St
State St
6
Tchoupitoulas St

Eleonore St
Nashville Ave
Arabella St

A **B** **C** **D**

For reviews see

⊙	Top Sights	p106
⊙	Sights	p114
⊗	Eating	p114
⊖	Drinking	p117
★	Entertainment	p118
⌂	Shopping	p118

0   500 m
0   0.25 miles

St Charles Ave/
Nashville Ave

St Charles Ave/
St Charles Jefferson Ave
Avenue
Streetcar

Milton H Latter
Memorial Library   Pitt St

UPTOWN

St Charles Ave/
Napoleon Ave

Sights

Newcomb Art Museum
MUSEUM

1 ⊙ MAP P112, D2

Part of Tulane University and flanked by beautiful Tiffany stained-glass triptychs, the Newcomb Art Museum is a great spot to soak up some art, with works from colonial portraiture to engravings by John James Audubon. Just outside is a pretty green, where students sunbathe, toss Frisbees and generally recede into the happiest rhythms of American higher ed. (📞504-865-5328; http://newcombartmuseum.tulane.edu; Woldenberg Art Center, Tulane University; admission free; ⊙10am-5pm Tue-Fri, 11am-4pm Sat)

Audubon Park
PARK

2 ⊙ MAP P112, C5

This lovely spot, riverside of St Charles Ave, is home to Audubon Zoo (p108). A 1.8-mile multi-use paved trail loops around the central golf course, unfurling beneath a shady canopy of live oaks. (⊙5am-10pm)

Milton H Latter Memorial Library
NOTABLE BUILDING

3 ⊙ MAP P112, F5

Poised elegantly above shady stands of palms, the Latter Memorial Library was once a private mansion. The Isaac family – who owned the building from 1907 to 1912 and installed Flemish-style carved woodwork, Dutch murals and French frescoed ceilings – passed the property to aviator Harry Williams and his silent-film-star wife, Marguerite Clark (1912–39). The next owner was local horse racer Robert S Eddy, followed by mr and Mrs Harry Latter, who gave the building to the city in 1948. (📞504-596-2625; www.nolalibrary.org; 5120 St Charles Ave; ⊙10am-8pm Mon-Thu, to 5pm Fri & Sat, 1-5pm Sun)

Eating

Boucherie
SOUTHERN US $$

4 ✖ MAP P112, C1

The thick, glistening cuts of bacon on the BLT can only be the work of the devil – or chef Nathanial Zimet, whose house-cured meats and succulent Southern dishes are lauded citywide. Savor boudin (Cajun sausage) balls with garlic aioli ($9), blackened shrimp in bacon vinaigrette, and smoked Wagyu-style brisket. The Krispy Kreme bread pudding with rum syrup ($7) is a wonder. (📞504-862-5514; www.boucherie-nola.com; 1506 S Carrollton Ave; mains lunch $12-23, dinner $18-30; ⊙11am-3pm Tue-Sat, 5:30-9:30pm Mon-Sat, 10:30am-2:30pm Sun)

Gautreau's
AMERICAN $$$

5 ✖ MAP P112, F4

There's no sign outside Gautreau's, just the number 1728 discreetly marking a nondescript house in a residential neighborhood. Cross the threshold to find a refined but welcoming dining room, where savvy diners, many of them New Orleanian food aficionados, enjoy fresh, modern American fare. (☏504-899-7397; www.gautreaus-restaurant.com; 1728 Soniat St; mains $30-45; ☺6-10pm Mon-Sat)

Clancy's
CREOLE $$$

6 ✕ MAP P112, C6

This white-tablecloth neighborhood restaurant embraces style, the good life and Creole cuisine with a chattering joie de vivre and top-notch service. The city's professional set comes here to gossip and savor the specialties: fried oysters and brie ($15), veal with crabmeat and béarnaise ($28), and lobster and mushroom risotto ($30). Reservations recommended. (☏504-895-1111; www.clancysneworleans.com; 6100 Annunciation St; mains lunch $17-20, dinner $28-40; ☺11:30am-1:30pm Thu & Fri, 5:30-10pm Mon-Sat)

Jacques-Imo's Café
LOUISIANAN $$

7 ✕ MAP P112, B1

Ask locals for restaurant recommendations in New Orleans, and almost everybody mentions Jacques-Imo's. We understand why: cornbread muffins swimming in butter, steak smothered in blue-cheese sauce, and the insane yet wickedly brilliant shrimp and alligator-sausage cheesecake. (☏504-861-0886; http://jacques-imos.com; 8324 Oak St; mains $20-34; ☺5-10pm Mon-Thu, to 11pm Fri & Sat)

Avo
SICILIAN $$

8 ✕ MAP P112, D5

Avo is a new kid on the Magazine St block, serving pastas cooked to perfection – as one would expect, with the owner-chef hailing from Sicily. It's clean, cozy, and convenient – a perfect stop if you're strolling along shopping and need a bite. They also offer impressive takes on classic cocktails and a 4pm-to-6pm happy hour (cocktails $6, wine half price). (☏504-509-6550; http://restaurantavo.com; 5908 Magazine St; mains $17-32; ☺4-10pm Mon-Thu, from 5pm Fri & Sat)

DTB
CAJUN $$$

9 ✕ MAP P112, B1

DTB is the new place on Oak everyone's talking about. Get melt-in-your-mouth meats, crisp salads, and creative takes on Cajun comfort food (roasted cauliflower, for instance, or stuffed banana beignets) in an airy spot finished with scrubbed steel, wood and marble – with Spanish moss hanging from the lamps. The cocktails, unique recipes crafted with care, are fun, inventive and refreshing. (Down The Bayou; ☏504 518-6889; http://dtbnola.com; 8201 Oak St; mains $25-35; ☺10:30am-2:30pm Fri-Sun, 5-10pm Sun-Thu, 5-11pm Fri & Sat)

Ba Chi Canteen
VIETNAMESE $

10 ✕ MAP P112, B2

Do not be skeptical of the 'bacos' ($3), as odd as they sound. These pillowy bundles of deliciousness

FOTOLUMINATE LLC/SHUTTERSTOCK ©

Audubon Park (p114)

(a *banh bao* crossed with a taco) successfully merge the subtle seasonings of Vietnamese fillings with the foldable convenience of a taco-shaped, steamed flour bun. (📞504-373-5628; www.facebook. com/bachicanteenla; 7900 Maple St; mains $4-12; ⏰11am-2:30pm Mon-Fri, to 3:30pm Sat, 5:30-9pm Mon-Wed, to 10pm Thu-Sat)

Pho Cam Ly
VIETNAMESE $

11 ⊗ MAP P112, H5

After much exhaustive research, this is our go-to bowl of pho in New Orleans (short of driving to New Orleans East). The Pho Cam Ly broth is rich and exciting and textured and makes you go all kinds of 'mmm'. There are plenty of excellent vermicelli bowls and

rice dishes if you're not in a soup mood. (📞504-644-4228; www. phocamly.com; 3814 Magazine St; mains $7-13; ⏰11am-8:30pm Mon-Sat, to 7:30pm Sun)

Cowbell
BURGERS $$

12 ⊗ MAP P112, B1

Cowbell has a scruffy charm – scuffed wooden floors, Elvis on the ceiling, a bottle-cap mosaic on one of its bars – that makes you want to stay awhile. The juicy grass-fed beef burgers are a must for most, but non-beef options include grilled Gulf fish tacos and lime-grilled organic chicken. We hear the mac 'n' cheese is divine. (www. cowbell-nola.com; 8801 Oak St; mains $12-32; ⏰11:30am-9pm Tue-Thu, to 10pm Fri & Sat)

Nomiya
JAPANESE $

13 ⊗ MAP P112, G6

Irasshaimase! That's what they yell whenever you enter a business in Japan, and it's what the servers say here as well. New Orleans has been in dire need of a good ramen place, and Nomiya has come to the rescue. Admire the comic-book and graffiti murals, then order your soup and add whatever extras you please. (www.nomiyaramen. com; 4226 Magazine St; ramen $13.50; ⏰11:30am-9:30pm Tue-Sun)

Wayfare
PUB FOOD $

14 ⊗ MAP P112, F3

This former takeout joint has gone all-in and now hovers in that delicious middle ground between pub (with inventive craft cocktails such as the Porkbelly Old Fashioned, garnished with a piece of bacon!) and restaurant (with a scrumptious eggplant-banh-mi sandwich that you wish you could take home to meet your parents). Either way, it's all about *yum*. (☑504-309-0069; www.wayfarenola.com; 4510 Freret St; mains $12-15; ☻11am-10pm Mon-Thu & Sat, to 11pm Fri, to 9pm Sun)

Creole Creamery ICE CREAM $

15 ☒ MAP P112, F5

Every single flavor here sounds – and is – uniquely delicious: Steen's Molasses Oatmeal Cookie; I Scream Fudge!; Pine Forest; Lavender Honey; Pear and Ginger Sorbet. And the list goes on. The good news is you can't go wrong. Flavors rotate, but there's always vanilla and chocolate, and you'll get in their Hall of Fame for eating eight scoops with eight toppings. (☑504-894-8680; www.creolecreamery.com; 4924 Prytania St; scoops $3; ☻noon-10pm Sun-Thu, to 11pm Fri & Sat)

Casamento's SEAFOOD $

16 ☒ MAP P112, G6

One word: oysters. That's why you come here. Walk through the 1949 soda-shop-esque interior, cross the tiled floors to a marble-top counter, trade a joke with the person shucking shells and get some raw boys with a beer. The thick gumbo with Creole tomatoes

and the oyster loaf (a sandwich of breaded and fried oysters) are suitably incredible. Cash only. (☑504-895-9761; www.casamentos-restaurant.com; 4330 Magazine St; mains $5-24; ☻11am-2pm & 5:30-9pm Thu-Sat, 5-9pm Sun)

Hansen's Sno-Bliz DESSERTS $

17 ☒ MAP P112, F6

The humble snowball (shaved ice with flavored syrup) is New Orleans' favorite dessert. Citywide consensus is that Hansen's, in business since 1939, does the best ball in town. Founder Ernest Hansen actually patented the shaved-ice machine. Now his granddaughter, Ashley, runs the family business, doling out shaved ice under everything from root-beer syrup to uber-popular Bananas Foster. (☑504-891-9788; www.facebook.com/snobliz; 4801 Tchoupitoulas St; snowballs $4-8; ☻1-7pm Tue-Sun Mar-Oct)

Drinking

Cure BAR

18 ☺ MAP P112, F3

This stylish purveyor of cocktails and spirits flickers like an ultra-modern apothecary shop, a place where mysterious elixirs are expertly mixed to soothe whatever ails you. A smooth and polished space of modern banquettes, anatomic art and a Zen-garden outdoor area, Cure is where you come for a well-mixed drink, period. It's drinks for adults in a stylish setting. (📞504-302-2357; www.curenola.com; 4905 Freret St; 🕑5pm-midnight Mon-Thu, 3pm-2am Fri & Sat, 3pm-midnight Sun)

Le Bon Temps Roulé BAR

19 🍷 MAP P112, F6

A neighborhood bar – a very good one at that – with a mostly college and post-college crowd attracted by two pool tables and a commendable beer selection. Late at night, high-caliber blues, zydeco or jazz rocks the joint's little back room. (📞504-897-3448; 4801 Magazine St; 🕑11am-3am)

Columns Hotel BAR

20 🍷 MAP P112, H4

With its antebellum trappings – a raised front porch, white Doric columns, a flanking live oak – the Columns Hotel harks back to a simpler era. But, truthfully, it's not as aristocratic as all that; it's more a place where college students and just-graduates drink beneath the grandeur of the Old South. (📞504-899-9308; www.thecolumns. com; 3811 St Charles Ave; 🕑3pm-midnight Mon-Thu, 11am-2am Fri & Sat, to midnight Sun)

St Joe's BAR

21 🍷 MAP P112, E5

New Orleanians have voted St Joe's the best in town several times. Patrons come to this dark-but-inviting place for the Japanese lantern decor, the well-used pool table, and the near-sacred jukebox.

(📞504-899-3744; www.stjoesbar. com; 5535 Magazine St; 🕑3pm-2am Sun-Thu, noon-3am Fri & Sat)

Entertainment

Tipitina's LIVE MUSIC

22 ⭐ MAP P112, G6

'Tips', as locals call it, is one of New Orleans' great musical icons. The legendary Uptown nightclub is the site of some of the city's most memorable shows, particularly when big names such as Dr John come home to roost. Outstanding music from local talent packs 'em in year-round. (📞504-895-8477; www.tipitinas.com; 501 Napoleon Ave; cover $5-20; 🕑8pm-2am)

Maple Leaf Bar LIVE MUSIC

23 ⭐ MAP P112, B1

The premier night-time destination in the Riverbend area, the legendary Maple Leaf's dimly lit, pressed-tin caverns are the kind of environs you'd expect from a New Orleans juke joint. The Grammy Award–winning Rebirth Brass Band plays Tuesdays, starting between 10pm and 11pm. (📞504-866-9359; www. mapleleafbar.com; 8316 Oak St; cover $10-20; 🕑3pm-2am)

Shopping

Yvonne La Fleur CLOTHING

24 🛍 MAP P112, B2

They don't make them like this anymore – neither the clothes, millinery, lingerie nor Yvonne herself, a businesswoman who has outfitted generations of local ladies for weddings, debuts and race days. Gentility, grace, style – thy name is Yvonne La Fleur. (☎504-866-9666; www.yvonnelafleur.com; 8131 Hampson St; ☺10am-6pm Mon-Wed, Fri & Sat, to 8pm Thu)

Peaches Records & Tapes
MUSIC

Peaches (☎16 Map p112, C6) has been around since 1975, doing the holy work of promoting, cataloging and marketing the best in local New Orleans music. It's a must see for anyone who wants to take home a piece of the city's musical heritage. (☎504-282-3322; www. peachesrecordsneworleans.com; 4318 Magazine St; ☺10am-7pm)

Potsalot
ARTS & CRAFTS

25 🔒 MAP P112, H5

Owners Alex and Cindy Williams, who have made and sold pottery from their Magazine St shop since 1993, call their exquisite creations functional art. Their unique, personally tested pieces, made for use in the kitchen, bathroom and den, include bowls, platters, lamps, vases and, yep, lotsa pots. (☎504-899-1705; www.potsalot.com; 3818 Magazine St; ☺10am-5pm Tue-Sat)

French Library
BOOKS

26 🔒 MAP P112, H5

This joli place is the largest French children's bookstore in the country. There are all kinds of lovingly bound titles, and the owners throw parties and private events for les

Uptown Shopping

Magazine St is the city's best shopping strip. You can take a good multi-mile window-shopping hike stretching from Audubon Park to Louisiana Ave. The area around Maple St in Riverbend is another hopping carnival of consumption.

enfants as well. (☎504-267-3707; www.thefrenchlibrary.com; 3811 Magazine St; ☺9am-6pm Tue-Sat, noon-5pm Sun)

Pied Nu
FASHION & ACCESSORIES

27 🔒 MAP P112, E6

If you need a hand-poured candle that lasts 60 hours, try one of the sweet-smelling Diptyques on sale here. As you soak up that vanilla-scented goodness, browse elephant-printed cotton T-shirt dresses, cinched poet-dresses and low-joe sneakers. (☎504-899-4118; www.piednuola.com; 5521 Magazine St; ☺10am-5pm Mon-Sat)

Hazelnut
HOMEWARES

Actor Bryan Batt of Mad Men fame co-owns this elegant, pleasantly eclectic gift and homewares shop (see 27 🔒 Map p112, E6). In addition to classically cool New Orleans–print toile, the shop sells gilded glassware, postmodern ceramics and other interior-decor must-haves for the stylishly modern. (☎504-891-2424; www.hazelnutneworleans.com; 5525 Magazine St; ☺10am-6pm Mon-Sat)

Explore

Mid-City, Bayou St John & City Park

Back in the day, this was the back of beyond: the bottom of the depression that is the New Orleans geographic bowl, an area of swampy lowlands and hidden gambler dens. Today? Mid-City and its adjacent neighborhoods form one of the loveliest residential areas in the city. This semiamorphous district includes long lanes of shotgun houses, bike lanes, the elegant mansions of Esplanade Ave and the slow, lovely, lazy Bayou St John.

A bike ride may be the most pleasant way to explore the 'green' sections of these neighborhoods. If you cycle independently, just roll up attractive Esplanade Ave (p126) and take it all the way to City Park (p122). Explore the park and the New Orleans Museum of Art (p126), and afterwards stop in for dinner at Café Degas (p129) or 1000 Figs (p129). In the evening, enjoy a drink at Pal's (p131).

Getting There & Around

🚋 The City Park spur of the Canal St streetcar line hits Carrollton St, then heads to City Park.

🚌 Bus 91 runs up Esplanade, and bus 27 follows Louisiana Ave, both to City Park. 94 runs along Broad St.

🚲 You can pedal up here via Esplanade Ave, which has a bicycle lane, or the Lafitte Greenway.

Neighborhood Map on p124

Mansion, Esplanade Avenue (p126) FOTOLUMINATE LLC/SHUTTERSTOCK ©

Top Sight
City Park

In many ways City Park is a near-perfect expression of a local 'park,' in the sense that it is an only slightly tamed expression of the forest and Louisiana wetlands (Bayou Metairie runs through the grounds) that are the natural backdrop of the city. Golf courses mar this narrative, but there's still enough wild to get lost in.

◉ **MAP P124, F2**

☎ 504-482-4888

www.neworleanscitypark.
com

Esplanade Ave & City
Park Ave

P 🚻 🐾

Botanical Gardens & Peristyle

The **Botanical Gardens** (📞504-483-9488; www.
neworleanscitypark.com/botanical-garden; City
Park; adult/child/under 3 $8/4/free; 🕙10am-5pm;
🅿) have been the site of many a New Orleans
wedding, and in their green depths you'll find
examples of flora from both around the world
and across the backyard of Louisiana.

Overlooking Bayou Metairie is the Peristyle
(p128; pictured left), a classical pavilion feat-
uring Ionic columns, built in 1907.

Theme Parks

Anyone who doesn't like the charmingly dated
Carousel Gardens (📞504-483-9402; www.ne-
worleanscitypark.com/in-the-park/carousel-gardens;
7 Victory Ave, City Park; adult/child 36in & under $4/
free, each ride $4; 🕙11am-6pm Sat & Sun Mar-May
& Aug-Oct, 11am-5pm Tue Fri, to 6pm Sat & Sun Jun
& Jul) must surely have a heart of stone. The
lovingly restored antique carousel is housed in
a 1906 structure with a stained-glass cupola.
In the 1980s, residents raised $1.2 million to
restore the broken animals, fix the squeaky mer-
ry-go-round and replace the Wurlitzer organ.

Storyland (http://neworleanscitypark.com/in-the-
park/storyland; 5 Victory Ave, City Park; adult/child 36in
& under $4/free; 🕙10am-5pm; ♿) doesn't have
rides, just fun statues of fairy-tale heroes and vil-
lains. If the characters seem strangely similar to
Mardi Gras floats, it's because they were created
by master float-builder Blaine Kern.

Couturie Forest

The wildest section of the park is this scad of
hardwood **forest** (Harrison Ave & Diagonal Dr;
admission free; 🕙sunrise-sunset; 🅿), where live
oaks shade leafy underbrush and mushrooms
peek out of the moist soil. Park your car in the
lot off the Harrison Ave traffic circle and you'll
see a road that extends back into the forest;
take any branching trail and get pleasantly lost.

★ Top Tips

● The best spots for
parking in City Park
include the area in
front of the New
Orleans Museum of
Art and the lot near
Morning Call.

● There are alligators
here! If you're walking
your dog or are near
the water, keep an eye
out. We're not kidding
– local gators aren't
common, but they're
not unheard of.

● The waters in the
park aren't suitable
for swimming. See
the above tip about
alligators.

✗ Take a Break

Near the sculpture
garden, take a
break for coffee and
beignets at **Morning
Call**. (http://ne-
worleanscitypark.com/
in-the-park/morning-
call; Dreyfous Ave, City
Park; mains $2-10;
🕙24hr)

Want a picnic lunch?
Head to **Canseco's**
(📞504-322-2594;
www.cansecos.com;
3135 Esplanade Ave;
hot plates $7-10;
🕙7am-10pm) on
Esplanade Ave and
grab something
from their hot bar.

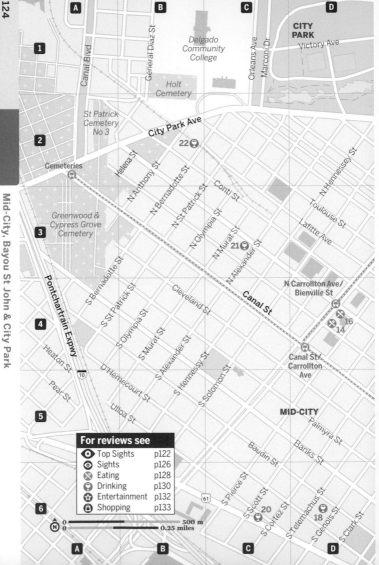

CITY PARK
Victory Ave

Delgado
Community
College

Canal Blvd

General Diaz St

Orleans Ave

Marconi Dr

Holt
Cemetery

St Patrick
Cemetery
No 3

City Park Ave

22

Cemeteries

Helena St

N Anthony St

N Bernadotte St

N St Patrick St

Conti St

N Olympia St

N Murat St

N Alexander St

N Hennessey St

Toulouse St

Lafitte Ave

Greenwood &
Cypress Grove
Cemetery

21

Pontchartrain Expwy

S Bernadotte St

S St Patrick St

Cleveland St

Canal St

N Carrollton Ave/
Bienville St

16
14

S Olympia St

S Murat St

S Alexander St

S Hennessy St

S Solomon St

Canal St/
Carrollton
Ave

Heaton St

D'Hemecourt St

MID-CITY

Palmyra St

Pear St

Ulloa St

Banks St

Baudin St

For reviews see

◎ Top Sights   p122
◎ Sights   p126
✗ Eating   p128
🍷 Drinking   p130
★ Entertainment   p132
🔒 Shopping   p133

S Pierce St

S Scott St

20

S Cortez St

S Telemachus St

18

S Genois St

S Clark St

0   500 m
0   0.25 miles

A   B   C   D

E

F

G

H

Sydney & Walda Besthoff Sculpture Garden

4 New Orleans Museum of Art

Wisner Blvd

St Louis Cemetery No 3 **6**

Belfort Ave **1**

ESPLANADE RIDGE

7 Peristyle

LeLong Dr

1

Fair Grounds Race Track

City Park

City Park & Museum of Art

Davis S

Allard Blvd

N Carrollton Ave

2 Bayou St John

5 Pitot House

Leda St

Esplanade Ave

?

Fortin St

10 23 Maurepas St

12 Ponce de

9 Leon St

Delgado Dr

Moss St

15

13

DAYOU ST JOHN

Grande Route St John

Esplanade Avenue

1

3

25

27

N Carrollton Ave/ Orleans Ave

Orleans Ave

Desoto St

Bell St

Bayou St John

Conti St

N Cortez St

Hagan Ave

N Rendon St

19

H Lopez St

N Salcedo St

N Gayoso St

St Philip St

Ursulines Ave

4

11

St Peter St

N Dupre St

Dumaine St

N Ann St

26

5

17

Bienville St

Iberville St

N Jefferson Davis Pkwy

Toulouse St

Lafitte Ave

N White St

N Broad St

Canal St/ Jefferson Davis Pkwy

6

N Dorgenois St

Canal St

S Jefferson Davis Pkwy

Cleveland St

S Rendon St

S Lopez St

S Salcedo St

S Gayoso St

S Dupre St

24

N Dupre St

N White St

Canal St/ White St

8

E

F

G

H

Sights

Sydney & Walda Besthoff Sculpture Garden

GARDENS

1 ⊙ MAP P124, E1

The sculpture garden that sits just outside the New Orleans Museum of Art is a wooded quilt of streams, pathways, lovers' benches and, of course, sculpture, mainly of the modern and contemporary sort. During spring and summer, theatrical productions are often put on here, but it's a lovely spot for a stroll any time of year. (www.noma.org/sculpture-garden; 1 Collins Diboll Circle; admission free; ⏱10am-6pm Apr-Sep, to 5pm Oct-Mar)

Bayou St John

RIVER

2 ⊙ MAP P124, F2

Back in the day, this was a true bayou – an overgrown morass of Spanish moss and prowling alligators. Native Americans, fur trappers and smugglers would use the waterway as a natural road that led over the dark wetlands to the shores of Lake Pontchartrain. Today, the bayou has been partially dredged and beautified into a narrow green space that makes for a breezy, altogether pleasant green ribbon that snakes across the center of the city. (Moss St & Wisner Ave; admission free; 🚼🐾)

Esplanade Avenue

STREET

3 ⊙ MAP P124, H3

Esplanade is one of the most beautiful streets in New Orleans, yet barely recognized by visitors as such. Because of the abundance of historical homes, Esplanade, which follows the 'high ground' of Esplanade Ridge, is known as the Creole St Charles Ave. Both streets are shaded by rows and rows of leafy live oaks, but whereas St Charles is full of large, plantation-style American villas, Esplanade is framed by columned, French Creole–style mansions. (btwn Rampart St & City Park)

New Orleans Museum of Art

MUSEUM

4 ⊙ MAP P124, E1

Inside City Park, this elegant museum was opened in 1911 and is well worth a visit for its special exhibitions, gorgeous marble atrium and top-floor galleries of African, Asian, Native American and Oceanic art. Its sculpture garden (p126) contains a cutting-edge collection in lush, meticulously planned grounds. Other specialties include Southern painters and an ever-expanding collection of modern and contemporary art. (NOMA; 📞504-658-4100; www.noma.org; 1 Collins Diboll Circle; adult/child 7-17yr $12/6; ⏱10am-6pm Tue-Thu, to 9pm Fri, 10am-5pm Sat, 11am-5pm Sun)

RAY LASKOWITZ/GETTY IMAGES ©

Bayou St John at dusk

Pitot House

HISTORIC BUILDING

5 ◉ MAP P124, F2

The Pitot House, perched prettily beside Bayou St John, is an excellent example of classical French New Orleans architecture. Constructed circa 1799, it's the only Creole Colonial house along the bayou that is open to the public. The shaded verandah served as a living area whenever the weather got too hot. The house is named for resident James Pitot, who served as first mayor of incorporated New Orleans and lived here from 1810 to 1819. Visitation is by guided tour. (☏504-482-0312; www.pitothouse.org; 1440 Moss St; adult/child under 12yr & senior $10/7; ◷10am-3pm Wed-Sat)

St Louis Cemetery No 3

CEMETERY

6 ◉ MAP P124, G1

This long but compact cemetery was established in 1854 at the site of the old Bayou Cemetery and is worth strolling through for a few minutes (longer if you're a cemetery enthusiast) Of particular note is the striking monument James Gallier Jr designed for his mother and father who were lost at sea. It's a few steps to the right just after you enter from Esplanade Ave. The cemetery's wrought-iron entrance gate is a beauty. (☏504-596-3050; 3421 Esplanade Ave; admission free; ◷9am-3pm Mon-Sat, to noon Sun)

History of the Bayou

Today, Bayou St John is a pleasant backdrop for a stroll or a short paddle in a kayak. But take a closer look. This sometimes smelly creek is the reason this city exists. It was originally used by Native Americans as a wet highway to the relatively high ground of Esplanade Ridge before French explorers realized the waterway was the shortest route between the Mississippi River – and by extension the Gulf of Mexico – and Lake Pontchartrain. It was essentially for this reason that New Orleans was built in its commanding position at the mouth of the Mississippi.

Eventually a canal built by Governor Carondelet extended the bayou to the edge of the French Quarter, and the bayou acted as the city's chief commercial harbor. Life in the area thrived; beautiful houses lined the bayou (many remain here today) and voodoo queen Marie Laveau and her followers supposedly conducted rituals on the waterfront.

The era of steamboats made direct navigation up and down the Mississippi easier and the bayou began to be eclipsed. Navigation ended with the filling of the canal in 1927, but the bayou remained an important geographic point of reference.

Peristyle

ARCHITECTURE

 7 ⊚ MAP P124, E1

This eye-catching pavilion in City Park, built in 1907, is marked by Ionic columns and flanked by four lions. It looks like it was summoned via some time machine from ancient Greece, but today it's a great spot to sit with a sweetie and watch the sun set. The structure was originally built for private events and many weddings happen here. (http://neworleanscitypark.com/rentals-and-catering/venues/peristyle; City Park; sunrise-sunset)

Eating

Marjie's Grill

ASIAN $$

8 ✖ MAP P124, G6

In one word: brilliant. Marjie's is run by chefs who were inspired by Southeast Asian street food, but rather than coming home and doing pale imitations of the real thing, they've turned an old house on Broad St into a corner in Hanoi, Luang Prabang or Chiang Mai. With that said, there's a hint of New Orleans at work. (☎504-603-2234; www.marjiesgrill.com; 320 S Broad St; mains $8-26; ⊙11am-2:30pm & 5:30-10pm Mon-Fri, 4-10pm Sat)

Liuzza's By The Track
DINER $

9 ⊗ MAP P124, H2

Mmmm, that gumbo. This quintessential Mid-City neighborhood joint does some of the best in town. The barbecue shrimp po'boy is to die for and the deep-fried garlic oysters are legendary. The atmosphere is unforgettable: we've seen a former city judge and a stripper dining together here, which is as 'Only in New Orleans' an experience as you can get. (☏504-218-7888; www.liuzzasnola.com; 1518 N Lopez St; mains $7-16; ⊙11am-7pm Mon-Sat)

1000 Figs
MIDDLE EASTERN $$

10 ⊗ MAP P124, H2

Although the menu isn't exclusively vegetarian, 1000 Figs serves our favorite vegetarian fare in town. The falafel, hummus, baba ghanouj and lentil soup are just good – freshly prepared and expertly executed. The dining space is well lit and seating makes you feel as if you're eating in a best friend's stylish dining room. (☏504-301-0848; www.1000figs.com; 3141 Ponce de Leon St; small plates $5-16; ⊙11am-9pm Tue-Sat; ☍)

Parkway Tavern
SANDWICHES $

11 ⊗ MAP P124, F4

Who makes the best po'boy in New Orleans? Honestly, who can say? But tell a local you think the top sandwich comes from Parkway and you will get, at the least, a nod of respect. The roast beef in particular – a craft some would say is dying among the great po'boy makers – is messy as hell and twice as good. (☏504-482-3047; www.parkwaypoorboys.com; 538 Hagan Ave; po'boys $8-14; ⊙11am-10pm Wed-Mon; P ☍)

Café Degas
FRENCH $$

12 ⊗ MAP P124, H3

A pecan tree thrusts through the floor and ceiling of the enclosed deck that serves as Café Degas' congenial dining room. A rustic, romantic little spot, Degas warms the heart with first-rate French fare. Meals that sound familiar on the menu – steak frites au poivre, parmesan-crusted veal medallions – are arranged with extraordinary beauty on the plate. (☏504-945-5635; www.cafedegas.com; 3127 Esplanade Ave; lunch $8-18, dinner $14-31; ⊙11am-3pm Wed-Fri, from 10:30am Sat & Sun, 5:30-10pm Wed-Sat, to 9.30pm Sun)

Toups' Meatery
LOUISIANAN $$

13 ⊗ MAP P124, E3

Cheese plates. Charcuterie boards. These are standard appetizers at restaurants across the land. But they are nothing compared to the chest-pounding glory that is the Toup's Meatery Board, a Viking-worthy platter of MEAT. House-made and cured, this carnivore's feast will harden your arteries in a single glance. But oh, that butter-soft marrow on the bone. (☏504-252-4999; www.toupsmeatery.com; 845 N Carrollton Ave; lunch $14-22, small plates $11-17, mains $22-34; ⏰11am-2:30pm Tue-Sat, 5-10pm Tue-Thu, 5-11pm Fri & Sat)

Angelo Brocato   ICE CREAM $

14 🍴 MAP P124, D4

When an ice-cream parlor passes the 100-year mark, you gotta step back and say, 'Clearly, they're doing something right.' Opened in 1905 by Signor Brocato himself, a Sicilian immigrant who scraped together his savings from working on a sugar plantation, this is the oldest ice-cream shop in New Orleans. Inside, silky gelatos, perfect cannoli and crispy biscotti wow the tastebuds. (☑504-486-0079; www.angelobrocatoicecream.com; 214 N Carrollton Ave; scoop of gelato $3.25, pastries under $4; ⏰10am-10pm Tue-Thu, to 10:30pm Fri & Sat, to 9pm Sun)

Lola's   SPANISH $$

15 🍴 MAP P124, G2

Enjoy wine and conversation with crowds of Mid-City locals who swear by Lola's paellas and *fideuàs* (an angel-hair pasta variation on the former). Inside, it's all elbows and the buzz of conversation and good grub. This isn't haute Barcelona cuisine; it's the Spanish peasant fare Hemingway wrote chapters about: rabbit, meats, fresh seafood, olive oil and lots of delicious garlic. (☑504-488-6946; www.lolasneworleans.com; 3312 Esplanade Ave; mains $13-34; ⏰5:30-9:30pm Sun-Thu, to 10pm Fri & Sat)

Bevi Seafood Co.   SEAFOOD $$

16 🍴 MAP P124, D4

Inside, Bevi's has less atmosphere than the moon, but if you don't mind the bare walls and cafeteria seating, there's excellent local seafood to be had, from boiled crawfish to head-on barbecue shrimp to a po'boy with fried oysters, melted Gouda cheese and bacon (!). (☑504-488-7503; http://beviseafoodco.com; 236 Carrollton Ave; mains $8-20; ⏰11am-8pm Tue-Sat, to 4pm Sun & Mon)

Katie's   CREOLE $$

17 🍴 MAP P124, E5

Katie's is how New Orleans does a family restaurant. Everything is taken over the top to new levels of decadent enjoyment; onion rings swim in remoulade sauce, fries are tossed with garlic butter and blue cheese, and the oysters Slessinger, doused in cheese, shrimp and bacon...oh wow. Portions are enormous. (☑504-488-6582; www.katiesinmidcity.com; 3701 Iberville St; mains $11-24; ⏰11am-9pm Mon-Thu, to 10pm Fri & Sat, 9am-3pm Sun; 👪)

Drinking

Twelve Mile Limit   BAR

18 🍸 MAP P124, D6

Twelve Mile is simply a great bar. It's staffed by people who have the skill, both behind the bar and in the kitchen, to work in four-star spots, but who chose to set up shop in a neighborhood, for a neighborhood. The mixed drinks are excellent, the match of any mixologist's cocktail in Manhattan, and the vibe is super accepting. (📞504-488-8114; www.facebook.com/twelve.mile.limit; 500 S Telemachus St; ⏰5pm-2am Mon-Thu, 11am-2am Fri, 10am-2am Sat, 10am-midnight Sun)

Pal's
BAR

19 🚌 MAP P124, G4

This great neighborhood bar is a little more convivial for the older generation, although it's definitely an all-ages crowd. The men's bathroom, wallpapered with vintage pinups, is like a walk through *Playboy's* history, while the backroom air hockey is always enjoyable. Open until at least 3am Sunday through Thursday and at least 4am on Friday and Saturday. (📞504-488-7257; www.palslounge.com; 949 N Rendon St; ⏰3pm-late)

Treo
COCKTAIL BAR

20 🚌 MAP P124, C6

My Whole Life Is Thunder. Shochu Wanna Party. The Rubio. Treo knows how to name a cocktail and, more importantly, how to mix one. Tipplers have a choice of seasonal drinks and Louisiana-style small plates. For a touch of culture, check out the art gallery upstairs. And that cool art piece on the ceiling? A wooden map of New Orleans. (📞504-304-4878, www.treonola.com; 3835 Tulane Ave; ⏰4pm-midnight)

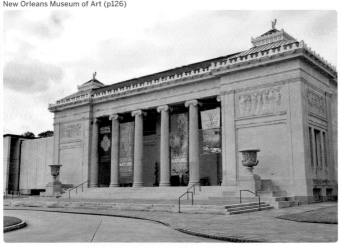

New Orleans Museum of Art (p126)

CHUCK WAGNER/SHUTTERSTOCK ©

JAIMIE TUCHMAN/SHUTTERSTOCK ©

Carousel Gardens (p123)

Station
CAFE

21 ⊕ MAP P124, C3

There are plenty of cafes in Mid-City, but Station is a significant caffeinated cut above the rest. The coffee is simply thoughtfully curated and brewed well; there's no need for crazy espresso concoctions here. Try the Vietnamese *cafe sua da* (iced coffee with condensed milk) – it's a treat on a hot day. (☑504-309-4548; www.thestation.coffee; 4400 Bienville St; ☺6:30am-8pm Mon-Fri, 7:30am-5pm Sat & Sun)

Second Line Brewing
BREWERY

22 ⊕ MAP P124, B2

Located at the end of some old railroad tracks, Second Line has turned a light industrial warehouse into a kicking brewery with a courtyard and kid-friendly play accoutrements. The frequent presence of food trucks makes this outdoor suds spot a popular place with families and those seeking beer and bites al fresco. (☑504-248-8979; www.secondline-brewing.com; 433 N Bernadotte St; ☺4-10pm Wed-Fri, noon-10pm Sat, to 8pm Sun; ⛹)

Fair Grinds
CAFE

23 ⊕ MAP P124, H2

Like many of the best indie coffee shops, Fair Grinds is comfy, hip and unpretentious. And, of course, it serves a good cup of joe. It also showcases local art and generally acts as the beating heart of Mid-City's bohemian scene; plus, it supports community development associations and hosts regular folk-music nights. (☑504-913-9072; 3133 Ponce de Leon St; ☺6:30am-9pm; 🛜)

Entertainment

Chickie Wah Wah
LIVE MUSIC

24 ⭐ MAP P124, F6

Despite the fact it lies in Mid-City on one of the most unremarkable stretches of Canal St, Chickie Wah Wah is a great music venue. Local legends, such as Sunpie Barnes and Alex McMurry, and plenty of international talent, all make their way across the small stage. (☑844-244-2543; www.chickiewahwah.com; 2828 Canal St;

cover $5-10; ⏱5pm-midnight Mon-Fri, 7pm-midnight Sat & Sun)

Shopping

Tubby & Coos   BOOKS

25 🔒 MAP P124, E3

Haven't found the droids you were looking for? Then stop by this self-proclaimed 'geeky' bookstore where books and movies loved by nerds take the spotlight. *Game of Thrones, Dr Who, Star Wars* – the gang is all here. They have a great kids section upstairs and rent out an enormous selection of board games. (📞504-598-5536; www.tubbyandcoos.com; 631 N Carrollton Ave; 10am-7pm Thu-Tue; 📶)

F&F Botanica
Spiritual Supply   GIFTS & SOUVENIRS

26 🔒 MAP P124, H5

Hesitant to enter a 'voodoo store'? Don't worry, staff couldn't be more helpful at this jam-packed shop that's lined with colorful candles. Forget all the fake voodoo shops in the French Quarter, this is a genuine Puerto Rican botanica that sells issue-related candles (success, love, etc), *gris-gris* (spell bags or amulets) and spell components. (📞504-482-9142; www.orleanscandleco.com; 801 N Broad Ave; ⏱8am-5pm Mon, Tue & Thu-Sat)

Home Malone   GIFTS & SOUVENIRS

27 🔒 MAP P124, E3

You won't find Macaulay Culkin or improvised booby traps here, but this lovely shop is packed with bath bombs, New Orleans-ish home decor and local original art. A perfect shop for a South Louisiana souvenir. (📞504-324-8352; https://homemalonenola.com; 629 N Carrollton Ave; ⏱10am-6pm Tue-Sat, noon-5pm Sun)

Explore ◈

Tremé-Lafitte

Few neighborhoods hold their finger on the city's cultural pulse like the Tremé. This handful of square blocks – arguably the oldest African American neighborhood in the country – has had a disproportionate impact on world music. This is where jazz was invented, by free people of color and the descendants of slaves, who mixed African rhythms with European syncopation and homegrown improvisation.

The historical core of the Tremé is the area between Rampart St, Claiborne Ave, St Bernard Ave and Basin St. Much of this real estate is taken up by Louis Armstrong Park (p138). Around here is where you'll find some of the most attractive streets in the neighborhood; the area where Gov Nicholls St intersects with Henriette DeLille St is particularly lovely.

Getting There & Around

🚌 The area is relatively well served by city-bus lines – buses 51, 52, 57 and 91 all pass through Tremé-Lafitte.

🚋 The Rampart Streetcar line runs along the edge of the neighborhood.

🚲 The Lafitte Greenway begins (or ends, depending on where you're coming from) here. Esplanade Ave has a bicycle lane.

Neighborhood Map on p136

Tremé-Lafitte

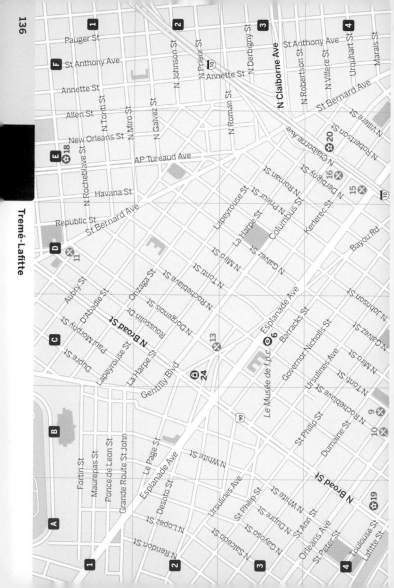

Pauger St

1

F St Anthony Ave

Annette St

Allen St

New Orleans St

E ⭐18

Havana St

Republic St

St Bernard Ave

D ✗11

Aubry St

Dupre St

Paul Murphy St

N Broad St

Gentilly Blvd

C

Esplanade Ave

B

Fortin St

Maurepas St

Ponce de Leon St

Grande Route St John

Le Page St

N White St

N Rendon St

N Lopez St

Desoto St

N Salcedo St

N Gayoso St

A

N Johnson St
N Prieur St
N Derbigny St
N Roman St
N Galvez St
N Miro St
N Tonti St
N Rocheblave St

2

3 St Anthony Ave

N Claiborne Ave
St Anthony Ave
N Robertson St
N Villere St
Urquhart St
Marais St

4

N Annette St
⚲10

AP Tureaud Ave

St Bernard Ave

N Villere St
N Robertson St

⭐20 N Claiborne Ave

✗16 N Derbigny St
N Roman St

🍴15

⚲10

Lapeyrouse St
La Harpe St
Columbus St
Kerlerec St

Bayou Rd

N Prieur St
N Galvez St

N Miro St

N Tonti St

N Rocheblave St
N Dorgenois St
N Rousselin Dr
D'Abadie St
Lapeyrouse St
La Harpe St

✗13

🅟24

Esplanade Ave
Barracks St

⚲6 Le Musée de t.p.c.

Governor Nicholls St
Ursulines Ave

St Philip St

N Johnson St
N Galvez St
N Miro St
N Tonti St
N Rocheblave St

✗9

Dumaine St
✗10

N Broad St

⭐19

Ursulines Ave
St Philip St
N Dupre St
St Ann St
N White St

Orleans Ave
St Peter St

Toulouse St
Lafitte St

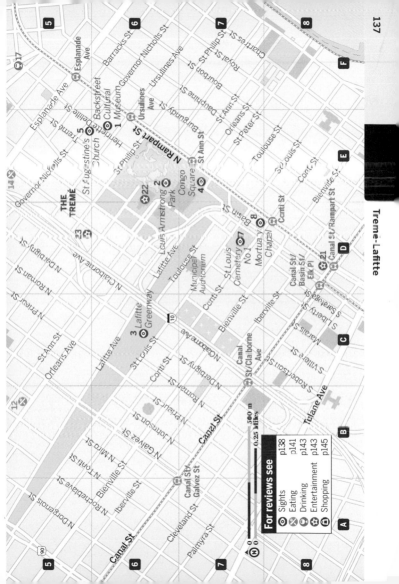

Treme-Lafitte

THE TREMÉ

Esplanade Ave

Backstreet Cultural Museum 1

Henriette Delille St

St Augustine's Church 5

Esplanade Ave

Treme St

Governor Nicholls St

Barracks St

Governor Nicholls St

Ursulines Ave

Ursulines Ave

St Philip St

Dumaine St

N Rampart St

St Philip St

St Ann St

Orleans Ave

St Ann St

St Peter St

Toulouse St

Bourbon St

Dauphine St

Royal St

Chartres St

Royal St

Chartres St

Louis Armstrong Park

Congo Square 4

22

2

St Louis St

Basin St

Conti St

Conti St

St Louis St

Bienville St

N Claiborne Ave

Lafitte Ave

Municipal St

Toulouse St

Conti St

St Louis Cemetery No 1 7

Mortuary Chapel

8

Canal St/ Basin St/ Elk Pl

Bienville St

Canal St Rampart St 21

33

Lafitte Greenway 3

Lafitte Ave

St Louis St

Conti St

N Derbigny St

Bienville St

Iberville St

10

Canal/ Claiborne Ave

St Canal/Claiborne Ave

S Saratoga St

S Liberty St

S Villere St

Conti St

N Derbigny St

N Prieur St

N Roman St

St Ann Ave

Orleans Ave

N Robertson St

S Robertson St

Tulane Ave

12

Canal St

500 m

0.25 Miles

Canal St/ Galvez St

Cleveland St

Palmyra St

Canal St

N Galvez St

N Johnson St

N Prieur St

N Roman St

N Tonti St

Bienville St

Iberville St

N Rocheblave St

N Dorgenois St

N Miro St

90

For reviews see

⊙ Sights   p138
✕ Eating   p141
🍷 Drinking   p143
★ Entertainment   p143
🛍 Shopping   p145

17

A B C D E F

5
6
7
8

Sights

Backstreet Cultural Museum
MUSEUM

1 ◉ MAP P136, E6

Mardi Gras Indian suits grab the spotlight with dazzling flair – and finely crafted detail – in this informative museum examining the distinctive elements of African American culture in New Orleans. The museum isn't terribly big (it's the former Blandin's Funeral Home), but if you have any interest in the suits and rituals of Mardi Gras Indians, as well as Second Line parades and Social Aid and Pleasure Clubs (the local African American community version of civic associations), you need to stop by.

The guided tours are usually great, but sometimes feel rushed, so be sure to ask lots of questions. Ask for information about upcoming Second Lines so you can check one out firsthand. (📞504-522-4806; www.backstreetmuseum.org; 1116 Henriette Delille St; $10; ⏰10am-4pm Tue-Sat)

Louis Armstrong Park
PARK

2 ◉ MAP P136, E6

The entrance to this massive park has got to be one of the greatest gateways in the US, a picturesque arch that ought rightfully to be the final set piece in a period drama about Jazz Age New Orleans. The original Congo Sq is here, as well as a **Louis Armstrong statue** (Louis Armstrong Park) and a **bust of Sidney Bechet**. The Mahalia Jackson Theater (p145) hosts opera and Broadway productions. The park often hosts live-music festivals throughout the year. (701 N Rampart St; ⏰sunrise-sunset)

Lafitte Greenway
PARK

3 ◉ MAP P136, C6

This 2.6-mile green corridor connects the Tremé to City Park via Bayou St John, traversing the length of the Tremé and Mid-City along the way. It's a bicycle- and pedestrian-friendly trail that follows the course of one of the city's oldest transportation paths – this was originally a canal and, later, a railroad.

Over the years, the railroad right-of-way became decrepit; it is hoped the thoughtfully landscaped Greenway will reverse the legacies of that blight. The trail includes a raised asphalt path, energy-efficient trail lighting and wheelchair-accessible curb ramps. Although the Greenway is well lit, exercise caution late at night. (N Alexander & St Louis to Basin & St Louis; admission free; ⏰24hrs; 🚻👶)

Congo Square
HISTORIC SITE

4 ◉ MAP P136, E7

In Louis Armstrong Park, Congo Sq was a Sunday gathering spot for slaves under the French Code Noir. For one day of the week, the enslaved could sing the songs and practice the cultural traditions of the continent they were exiled from. This was the groundwork of a uniquely New Orleanian link to Africa and much of the city's most iconic food, music and culture has been built on that foundation.

Today Congo Sq is marked by a few stylized statues and sculptures of the city's musical heritage and heroes. The space is also a major jumping-off point for protest marches, rallies and Second Lines. (Louis Armstrong Park; admission free; ☺sunrise sunset)

St Augustine's Church CHURCH

5 ◉ MAP P136, E5

Open since 1841, 'St Aug's' is the oldest African American Catholic church in the country, a place where Creoles, émigrés from St Domingue and free persons of color could worship shoulder to shoulder, even as separate pews were designated for slaves. Call ahead to see if it's possible to arrange a visit. Don't miss the Tomb of the Unknown Slave, fashioned to resemble a grim cross assembled from chain links. (☎504-525-5934; www.staugchurch.org; 1210 Governor Nicholls St; ☺Mass 10am Sun, 5pm Wed)

Le Musée de f.p.c. MUSEUM

6 ◉ MAP P136, C3

Inside a lovely 1859 Greek Revival mansion in the Upper Tremé, this museum showcases a 30-year collection of artifacts, documents, furniture and art. It tells the story of a forgotten subculture: the 'free people of color' before the Civil War, who played a unique but

Jazz choir, St Augustine's Church

ANEESE/SHUTTERSTOCK ©

Mahalia Jackson Theater (p145)

prominent role in the development of the city. Visitation is by guided tour, which should be arranged in advance.

Rooms spotlight different eras in the city's history, with a focus on physician and newspaper publisher Dr Louis Charles Roudanez, born in 1823. The small but fascinating collection includes original documentation of slaves who became free, either by *coartación* (buying their own freedom) or as a reward for particularly good service. (Free People of Color Museum; 504-323-5074; www.le-museedefpc.com; 2336 Esplanade Ave; tour regular/private $15/25; tours 1-4pm Tue-Fri)

St Louis Cemetery No 1

CEMETERY

7 ⊙ MAP P136, D7

This cemetery received the remains of many early Creoles who were buried above-ground in family tombs due to the shallow water table. Cemetery visitation is limited to relatives of the interred and approved tours, which can be arranged via Save Our Cemeteries (p19) and booked via that organization's website. (504-596-3050; www.saveourcemeteries. org/st-louis-cemetery-no-1; 425 Basin St; guided tour adult/child $20/free; tours 10am, 11:30am & 1pm Mon-Sat, 10am Sun)

Mortuary Chapel
CHURCH

8 ◉ MAP P136, D7

A fear of yellow-fever contagion led the city to forbid funerals for fever victims at St Louis Cathedral. Built in 1826 near St Louis Cemetery No 1, the Mortuary Chapel offered services for victims, its bell tolling constantly during epidemics. In 1931 it was renamed Our Lady of Guadalupe. Inside the chapel is a statue of St Jude, patron saint of impossible cases. (Our Lady of Guadalupe; ☏504-525-1551; www.judeshrine.com; 411 N Rampart St; donations accepted; ☺Mass 7am & noon Mon-Fri, 7am & 4pm Sat, 7:30am, 9:30am, 11:30am & 1:30pm Sun)

Eating

Willie Mae's
Scotch House
SOUTHERN US $$

9 ✖ MAP P136, B4

Willie Mae's has been dubbed the best fried chicken in the world by the James Beard Foundation, the Food Network and other media, and in this case, the hype isn't far off – this is superlative fried bird. The white beans are also amazing. The drawback is everyone knows about it, so you should expect long lines, sometimes around the block. (☏504-822-9503; www.williemaesnola.com; 2401 St Ann St; fried chicken $15; ☺10am-5pm Mon-Sat)

Gabrielle
CAJUN $$

10 ✖ MAP P136, B4

This old school, high-end Cajun spot has been refurbished into a lovely little blue-and-yellow cottage doling out sumptuous, rich plates of braised rabbit, slow-roasted duck and other favorites. The wine list is deep and, all in all, this is a perfect spot for a date. (☏504-603-2011; 2111 Orleans Ave, mains $16-32; ☺5:30-10pm Tue-Sat)

Buttermilk Drop
BAKERY $

11 ✖ MAP P136, D1

You came to New Orleans and thought, 'I have to get beignets,' right? And sure, beignets are fine, but the best dessert in town is the buttermilk drop – a small donut hole filled with roughly a metric ton of butter, so rich and smooth and glazed and good it haunts our dreams.

Buy your drops at this ramshackle bakery, which has dusty floors and barely anything that qualifies as seating (get the food to go), and know you have experienced culinary bliss. (☏504-252-4538; www.buttermilkdrop.com; 1781 N Dorgenois St; baked goods $1-4; ☺6am-4pm Mon-Sat, to 3pm Sun)

Dooky Chase
CREOLE $$

12 ✖ MAP P136, B5

Ray Charles wrote 'Early in the Morning' about Dooky's; civil rights leaders used it as informal headquarters in the 1960s; and

Barack Obama ate here after his inauguration. Leah Chase's labor of love is the backbone of the Tremé and her buffets are the stuff of legend, a carnival of gumbo and fried chicken served in a white-linen dining room.

These days the food can be a little hit and...well, not miss, but not as much of a hit as it has been in the past. The vegetarian gumbo z'herbes, served on Thursday during Lent, is the great New Orleans dish done green with mustards, beet tops, spinach, kale, collards and Leah knows what else; committed carnivores should give it a try. (☏504-821-0600; www.dookychaserestaurant.com; 2301 Orleans Ave; buffet $20, mains $20-25; ⏱11am-3pm Tue-Thu, 11am-3pm & 5-9pm Fri)

Pagoda Cafe
CAFE $

13 ❌ MAP P136, C2

In a land of dimly lit dive bars and heavy Creole buffets, Pagoda Cafe is a sprightly diversion. This compact place serves healthy fare with a global spin. In the morning, try bacon-and-egg tacos, toast with Nutella and bananas, and housemade granola. For lunch to-go, grab a turnover or sausage pastry or settle in for a lemongrass tofu *banh mi*.

Also sells coffee and teas. All seating is outdoors. (☏504-644-4178; www.pagodacafe.net; 1430 N Dorgenois St; breakfast $3-9, pastries under $5, sandwiches $8-10;

⏱7:30am-3pm Tue-Fri, 8am-3pm Sat & Sun; 🛜🍴)

Lil' Dizzy's
CREOLE $

14 ❌ MAP P136, E5

One of the city's great lunch spots, Dizzy's does mean soul food specials in a historic shack owned by the Baquet family, who have forever been part of the culinary backbone of New Orleans. The fried chicken is excellent and the bread pudding is divine. (☏504-569-8997; www.lildizzyscafe.com; 1500 Esplanade Ave; breakfast $7-14, lunch $11-16, buffet $16-18; ⏱7am-2pm Mon-Sat, 8am-2pm Sun)

Manchu
AMERICAN, CHINESE $

15 ❌ MAP P136, E4

Also known as the 'purple shop' (when you see it, you'll know why), Manchu is a dingy little takeout that is most famous for its fried chicken wings. You can also pick up fried seafood, grilled pork chops and bowls of yakamein – a sort of black New Orleans version of *pho*, renowned for its hangover-curing powers.

This place is ostensibly Chinese – they sell Chinese staples such as fried rice and egg rolls – but the dishes that will draw you in are New Orleans soul food. (☏504-947-5507; www.manchuchicken.com; 1413 N Claiborne Ave; mains $5-12; ⏱10:30am-9pm Mon-Sat, 11:30am-7pm Sun)

Cajun Seafood   SEAFOOD $

16 MAP P136, E4

The name says it all: this is a grocery store—takeout that's a good budget option for seafood and cooked hot plates, such as fried chicken, boudin, fish plates and the like. The boiled shrimp is always freakishly huge, as are the shrimp po'boys. (📞504-948-6000; http://cajunseafoodnola.com; 1479 N Claiborne Ave; takeout $5-19; ⏰10:30am-8:30pm Mon-Sat, from 11am Sun)

Drinking

Sidney's Saloon   BAR

17 🍺 MAP P136, F5

Friendly bartenders, strong drinks, pop-up restaurants slinging food on the nearby street and a raucous clientele make Sidney's a winning stop any night of the week. Hosts trivia nights on Tuesdays, comedy on Thursdays and dance parties on the weekend. (📞504-224-2672; www.sidneyssaloon.com; 1200 St Bernard Ave; ⏰3pm-3am)

Entertainment

Bullets   LIVE MUSIC

18 ⭐ MAP P136, E1

Don't be put off by the name; Bullets is just a sports bar. Well, sort of – this is New Orleans, so it's a sports bar, but a sports bar where live music kicks off on a regular basis. The crowd is friendly, the beer

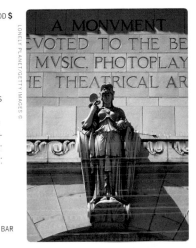

LONELY PLANET/GETTY IMAGES ©

Saenger Theatre (p145)

is cold, the drinks are strong and the music is good – what more do you want? (📞504-948-4003; 2441 AP Tureaud Ave; cover $5; ⏰bar 7am-2am, shows 6pm & 9pm)

Broad Theater   CINEMA

19 ⭐ MAP P136, A4

The Broad is a great movie theater, showcasing both Hollywood blockbusters and indie/art house titles in the middle of the city. It's extremely popular with locals, and during busy shows, the parking lot is almost always full to capacity, so you may want to seek out street parking. The on-site bar certainly helps with your cinematic relaxation. (636 N Broad St; ⏰1pm-midnight Mon-Wed, from 11am Thu-Sun)

Throwing a Second Line
at the Drop of a Hat

Second Lines aren't the alternative queue at the bank window, if you're wondering. No, Second Line specifically refers to New Orleans neighborhood parades, especially those put on by the city's African American Social Aid and Pleasure (S&P) Clubs. The S&P members deck themselves out in flash suits, hats and shoes and carry decorated umbrellas and fans. This snazzy crowd, accompanied by a hired band, marches through the city pumping music and 'steppin' – engaging in a kind of syncopated marching dance that looks like a soldier in formation overcome by an uncontrollable need to get fun-kay.

This is the First Line and marching behind it is the Second Line: the crowds that gather to celebrate the music. Hundreds, sometimes thousands of people – the majority African American – dance in the Second Line, stopping for drinks and food all along the parade route. Many folks bring along coolers full of beer and soda, plus rolling grills, too.

So what are these S&P clubs? There are theories they have their roots in West African secret societies, cultural institutions that were a big part of the societies slaves were plucked from. While this theory has an appealing veneer of anthropological allure, the origins of Second Lines may be more based on economics. In the 19th and 20th centuries, S&P clubs functioned as insurance agencies for African Americans, as well as brokers who would help arrange the traditional (and expensive) New Orleans jazz funeral procession. The act of the parade, which the S&P helped fund, may have been eventually appended to these brokerage responsibilities.

While that role has faded, the S&P clubs remain important civic institutions. There are a few dozen in the city, and traditionally Second Lines roll every weekend, except for summers, usually in the Tremé or Central City. They're not the easiest thing to find, but keep abreast of 90.7 WWOZ's Takin' it To The Streets section (www.wwoz. org) or stop by the Backstreet Cultural Museum (p138) to ask – and be on the lookout for parades and music if you're driving around on a Sunday.

Also note that folks here will throw a Second Line for just about any reason. There were huge parades thrown to honor Fats Domino, Prince and David Bowie when those artists died, or to protest against Donald Trump and the city's Confederate monuments. Other Second Lines have celebrated marriages or anniversaries.

Kermit's Treme Mother in Law Lounge LOUNGE

20 ⭐ MAP P136, E4

Owned by iconic trumpeter Kermit Ruffins, this wonderfully odd bar is a Tremé standby and a popular spot for drinks during Second Lines. Or any time of day, really. Look for the big, bright building with lots of murals. Kermit himself is often dishing out free food at night.

This was formerly K-Doe's Mother in Law Lounge, owned by the late, great Ernie K-Doe. Besides being famous for writing the song 'Mother in Law,' Ernie would frequently proclaim his 'Emperorship of the Universe.' (📞504-975-3955; www.kermitstrememotherinlawlounge. com; 1500 N Claiborne Ave; ⏱10am-midnight)

Saenger Theatre THEATER

21 ⭐ MAP P136, D8

The Saenger's ornate 1927 facade was designed by noted New Orleans architect Emile Weil. It has been refurbished and renovated into one of the finest indoor venues in the city. Shows range from comedy slams to off-Broadway hits. (📞504-525-1052; www.saenger-nola.com; 1111 Canal St)

Mahalia Jackson Theater THEATER

22 ⭐ MAP P136, E6

Named for New Orleans' own Queen of Gospel, the Mahalia Jackson is one of the city's major main-stage venues. It often features performances ranging from ballet to stand-up comedy to classical music. (📞504-287-0350; www.mahaliajacksontheater.com; 1419 Basin St)

Candlelight Lounge LIVE MUSIC

23 ⭐ MAP P136, D5

This classic Tremé dive is a hit-or-miss experience. Great bands play here. Corey Henry and the Treme Brass Band, to name a few – and on some nights the music infuses the place and everything is magic. On other nights the bands clearly phone it in and the whole experience is overpriced.

We've had good nights here, and it's a popular spot on the Second Line routes, but fair warning, the Candlelight does not always shine. (📞504-525-4748; 925 N Robertson St; cover $10; ⏱11am-late)

Shopping

Kitchen Witch BOOKS

24 🔒 MAP P136, C2

At a time when stores are becoming more and more homogeneous, Kitchen Witch is doing its own thing, selling antique and vintage cookbooks to a loving clientele who are dedicated to this niche of the written word. Some of these cookbooks are true works of art; others are fascinating collector's items. All have a gastronomic story. (📞504-528-8382; http://kwcookbooks.com; 1452 N Broad St; ⏱11am-5:30pm)

Survival Guide

View of the New Orleans skyline from the Mississippi River
ALLARD ONE/SHUTTERSTOCK ©

Before You Go

Book Your Stay

Where you stay in
New Orleans depends
largely on why you've
come here. You can
shell out some cash
for top accommoda-
tions and play the
whole time in the
French Quarter, or
experience the softer
(but still fun) side of
the city via one of its
many quirky B&Bs.
There are many
options on offer; the
city's one weakness is
a lack of backpacker
hostels.

Useful Websites

○ **New Orleans Online**
(www.neworleanson-
line.com/book) Official
tourism website for
the city.

○ **Louisiana Bed &
Breakfast Associa-
tion** (www.louisiana-
bandb.com) Direc-
tory of local B&Bs and
guesthouses.

○ **New Orleans Hotels**
(www.bestneworleans-
hotels.com) Has
some links to private
home rentals, as well

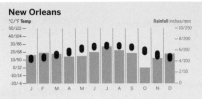

When to Go

Spring Mid-March
to late May is
the sweet spot.
Although you may
have to endure
some extremely hot
days, in general the
weather is pleasant
for shorts and shirt
sleeves. Plus, April
is the beginning
of music-festival
season!

Fall By October,
the weather begins
to cool off from the
long, long sum-
mer, and odd little
festivals and events
pop up around
town. Halloween is
an especially good
time for costumes,
weirdness and
debauchery.

as national chains.

○ **Lonely Planet**
(http://www.lone-
lyplanet.com/usa/
new-orleans/hotels)
A comprehensive, cu-
rated list of properties.

Best Budget

○ **Bywater Bed &
Breakfast** (☑504-944-
8438; www.bywaterbnb.
com; 1026 Clouet St; r
without bath $100-150; ☏)
Occupies the golden
mean between funky
and cozy.

○ **India House Hostel**
(☑504-821-1904; www.
indiahousehostel.com; 124

S Lopez St; dm $22-26, d/q
$50/99; ☻❄@☏☲)
Well-run hostel with a
fun clientele.

○ **City House Hostel**
(☑504-571-9854; www.
cityhousehostels.com; 129 Burgundy
St; dm $21-28, d $165;
☻❄☏) You can't beat
the location of this
spotless hostel within
the French Quarter.

○ **Lookout Inn of New
Orleans** (☑504-947-
8188; www.lookoutne-
worleans.com; 833 Poland
Ave; d $99; ☏☲☳)
Wonderfully weird
outpost in bohemian
Bywater.

Best Midrange

○ **La Belle Esplanade**
(📞504-301-1424; www.
labelleesplanade.com; 2216
Esplanade Ave; r incl breakfast $190-230; 😊❄️🛜)
Gorgeous historical
home managed by an
original New Orleans
character.

○ **Cornstalk Hotel**
(📞504-523-1515; www.
cornstalkhotel.com; 915
Royal St; r $228-319;
🅿️❄️🛜) Famous for
its gate, the Cornstalk
is stately and well
located.

○ **Dauphine House**
(📞504-940-0943; www.
dauphinehouse.com; 1830
Dauphine St; d $125; 🛜)
An elegant B&B with
good service in the
Marigny.

○ **Olivier House** (📞504-
525-8456; www.olivier-
house.com; 828 Toulouse St;
d $229; ❄️🛜🏊) Return
guests love this spot
for its solid rooms and
attentive staff.

○ **Columns Hotel**
(📞504-899-9308; www.
thecolumns.com; 3811 St
Charles Ave; r $165-288;
😊❄️@🛜) Slightly
worn grandeur at a
historic mansion off St
Charles Ave.

○ **Pierre Coulon Guest
House** (📞504-250-0965;
www.pierrecoulonguest-
house.com; 714 Spain St; r

1-2 person $150, 3/4 person
$225/300; 🛜) A little
eccentric, but with a
whole lot of character.

Best Top End

○ **Audubon Cottages**
(📞504-561-5858; www.
auduboncottages.com; 509
Dauphine St; cottages $350-
1200; 🅿️😊❄️🛜🏊)
Gorgeous Creole
suites in the French
Quarter.

○ **Ace Hotel** (📞front
desk 504-900-1180, reservations 504-941-9191; www.
acehotel.com/neworleans;
600 Carondelet St; d
$300-360, ste $500-1100;
😊❄️🛜🏊🐾) A bas-
tion of contemporary
cool in the CBD.

○ **Saint** (📞504-522-
5400; www.thesaintho-
telneworleans.com; 931
Canal St; r/ste $242/874;
😊❄️@🛜) Sleek
and stylish accom-
modations that are
near heavenly, pun
intended.

○ **Roosevelt New
Orleans** (📞504-648-
1200; www.therooseveltne-
worleans.com; 123 Baronne
St; r $259-309, ste $329-
2000; 🅿️😊❄️@🛜🏊)
Legendary retreat with
a block-long lobby and
Sazerac Bar.

○ **Le Pavillon** (📞504-
581-3111, reservations

844-656-8636; www.
lepavillon.com; 833 Poydras
Ave; r $233-260, ste $599-
699; 🅿️😊❄️🛜🏊)
Old-school historical
beauty with modern
luxury amenities.

Arriving in New Orleans

Louis Armstrong New Orleans International Airport (MSY)

Located 13 miles west
of New Orleans. A taxi
to the CBD costs $36,
or $15 per passenger
for three or more pas-
sengers. Shuttles to
the CBD cost $24/44
per person one way/
return. Bus E2 takes
you to Carrollton and
Tulane Ave in Mid-City
for $2. It's about a
five-minute walk to
the airport rental-car
facility from the main
terminal.

Amtrak & Greyhound

Located adjacent to
each other downtown
on Loyola Ave at the

Union Passenger Terminal. You can walk to the CBD or French Quarter, but don't do so at night, or with heavy luggage. A taxi from here to the French Quarter should cost around $10; going further afield, you'll be pressed to spend more than $20.

Getting Around

Streetcar

Streetcars (aka trolleys or trams) have made a comeback in New Orleans, with four lines serving key routes in the city. They are run by the Regional Transit Authority (www.norta.com). Fares cost $1.25 – have exact change – or you can purchase a Jazzy Pass (one-/three-/five-/31-day unlimited rides $3/9/15/55), which is also good on buses. Jazzy Passes can be purchased from streetcar conductors, bus drivers, in Walgreens drugstores, from ticketing

machines at RTA shelters along Canal St, and via an online app. Streetcars run about every 15 to 20 minutes, leaning toward every 20 minutes (or more) later at night.

Bicycle

Cyclists will find New Orleans flat and relatively compact; however, heavy traffic, potholes, narrow roads and unsafe neighborhoods present some negatives to cycling, and fat tires are a near necessity. Oppressive summer heat and humidity also discourage a lot of cyclists. Buses are now equipped with bike racks. Only folding bicycles are permitted on streetcars. The city operates a fleet of **Blue Bikes** (☏504-608-0603; http://nola.socialbicycles.com; per hr $8) for rent. You can also find private bicycle rental outfits across town.

Bus

The Regional Transit Authority (www.norta.com) offers bus and streetcar services. Service is decent, but we wouldn't recommend relying solely on public transport during

a New Orleans visit, especially if you're staying longer than a few days. Fare is $1.25 plus 25¢ per transfer.

Car

Having your own car or renting one in New Orleans can make it much easier to fully experience the entire city, from Faubourg Marigny up to Riverbend, and out along Esplanade Ave. If you are planning to spend most of your time in the French Quarter, though, don't bother. You'll just end up wasting money on parking. Enforcement of parking fees is particularly efficient in the French Quarter, the CBD and the Warehouse District.

Essential Information

Accessible Travel

New Orleans is somewhat lax in this department. Sidewalk curbs rarely have ramps, and many historic public buildings and hotels are not equipped to meet the needs of wheelchair-users. Modern hotels adhere to standards established by the federal Americans with Disabilities Act by providing ramps, elevators and accessible bathrooms.

Red streetcars on the Canal St, Rampart Riverfront and Loyola–UPT Streetcar lines are accessible to riders with disabilities. The green streetcars that run along St Charles Ave are protected from changes by the National Register of Historic Places and have not been made accessible (www.norta.com/Accessibility.aspx). Regional Transit Authority buses offer a lift service; for information about paratransit service (alternative transportation for those who can't ride regular buses), call **RTA Paratransit** (📞 504-827-7433; www.norta.com/Accessibility/Paratransit).

Business Hours

New Orleans maintains business hours similar to much of the rest of the USA, except when it comes to bars.

Banks 9am to 5pm Monday to Thursday, 10am to 5:30pm Friday. Some branches are open 9am to noon Saturday.

Bars Usually 5pm until around 2am on weekdays and 3am or 4am on weekends. Many bars stay open indefinitely, but on the flip side, they'll often close if business is slow.

Post offices 8:30am to 4:30pm Monday to Friday and 8:30am to noon Saturday.

Restaurants 10am or 11am to 11pm (sometimes with a break from 2pm to 5pm); usually closed Sunday and/or Monday.

Stores 10am to 7pm or 8pm.

Discount Cards

The New Orleans pass (adult/child from $69/49) is a discount card that scores you either free or discounted admission at over 25 sights and tours, including the New Orleans Museum of Art, the Audubon Aquarium and Mardi Gras World. The pass can be purchased and downloaded online (www.neworleanspass.com).

Electricity

The electrical current in the USA is 110V to 115V, 60Hz AC. Outlets may be suited to flat two-prong (not grounded) or three-prong (grounded) plugs. If your appliance is made for another electrical system, you will need a transformer or adapter; if you didn't bring one along, buy one at any consumer-electronics store around town.

Type A
120V/60Hz

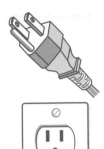

Type B
120V/60Hz

Emergency & Important Numbers

Ambulance ☏911

Fire ☏911

National Sexual Assault Hotline ☏800-656-4673

Police (emergency) ☏911

Police (nonemergency) ☏504-821-2222

Insurance

Foreign travelers may want to purchase health insurance before visiting the USA, as the cost of healthcare can be prohibitive (a single hospital visit can run to thousands of dollars). Other forms of insurance can cover the cost of changing tickets in the event of unforeseen developments during your trip.

Worldwide travel insurance is available at www.lonelyplanet.com/travel-insurance. You can buy, extend and claim online anytime – even if you're already on the road.

Media

Newspapers

Gambit (www.bestofneworleans.com) Weekly publication that covers arts, culture and music.

The Times-Picayune (www.nola.com) Broadsheet news and arts coverage three times a week.

The Advocate (www.theadvocate.com/new_orleans) More broadsheet news and culture writing.

New Orleans Magazine (www.myneworleans.com/new-orleans-magazine) Monthly focus on city society.

The Lens (http://thelensnola.org)

Investigative journalism and culture coverage; online only.

Radio

88.3 WRBH Reading radio for the blind.

89.9 WWNO NPR (National Public Radio).

90.7 WWOZ Louisiana music and community radio.

91.5 WTUL Tulane radio.

93.3 WQUE Hip-hop and R&B.

96.3 Classic hip-hop and R&B.

102.3 WHIV Music and community radio with an activist bent.

Post

New Orleans' main post office is near City Hall at 701 Loyola Ave. There are smaller branches throughout the city, including in the CBD at Lafayette Sq (9am to 1pm and 2pm to 5pm Monday to Friday) and Uptown Station at 2000 Louisiana Ave (8am to 4:30pm Monday to Friday and 8am to noon Saturday).

There are lots of independent postal shops as well, such as Fedex and the French Quarter Postal Emporium. These shops will send letters and packages at the same rates as the post office.

Toilets

A recording by Benny Grunch, 'Ain't No Place to Pee on Mardi Gras Day,' summarizes the situation in the French Quarter. While tour guides delight in describing the unsanitary waste-disposal practices of the old Creole days, the stench arising from back alleys is actually more recent in origin.

Public rest rooms can be found in the Jackson Brewery mall and in the French Market. Larger hotels often have accessible rest rooms off the lobby, usually near the elevators and pay phones.

Tourist Information

Right next to popular Jackson Sq in the heart of the French Quarter, the **New Orleans Welcome Center** (504-568-5661; www.crt.state.la.us/tourism; 529 St Ann St; 8:30am-5pm) in the lower Pontalba Building offers maps, listings of upcoming events and a variety of brochures for sights, restaurants and hotels. The friendly staff can help you find accommodations in a pinch, answer questions and offer advice about New Orleans.

Information kiosks scattered through main tourist areas offer most of the same brochures as the Welcome Center, but their staff tend to be less knowledgeable.

Order or download a Louisiana-wide travel guide online from the Louisiana Office of Tourism (www.louisianatravel.com).

In the Tremé, you can pick up a New Orleans map and look at displays about city attractions at the **Basin St Visitors Center** (504-293-2600; www.basinststation.com; 501 Basin St; 9am-5pm) inside Basin St Station.

Otherwise, **New Orleans Convention & Visitors Bureau** (CVB; 504 566-5011; www.neworleans.com; 2020 St Charles Ave; 8:30am-5pm) has plenty of free maps and helpful information

Volunteering

Literally hundreds of volunteer organizations descended upon New Orleans after Hurricane Katrina. Some did fantastic work; some acted with arrogance and left a sour taste. Almost everyone agrees that **Common Ground Relief** (504-312-1729; www.commongroundrelief.org; 1800 Deslonde St) is one of the better organizations in New Orleans – it works with locals, is committed to best practices and has a good track record in town.

Index

See also separate subindexes for:

- Eating p156
- Drinking p157
- Entertainment p157
- Shopping p158

🛍 Shopping

Behind the Scenes

Send Us Your Feedback

We love to hear from travelers – your comments help make our books better. We read every word, and we guarantee that your feedback goes straight to the authors. Visit **lonelyplanet.com/contact** to submit your updates and suggestions.

Note: We may edit, reproduce and incorporate your comments in Lonely Planet products such as guidebooks, websites and digital products, so let us know if you don't want your comments reproduced or your name acknowledged. For a copy of our privacy policy visit lonelyplanet.com/privacy.

Acknowledgements

Cover photograph: Royal St, French Quarter, Jason Langley/Getty ©

Adam's Thanks

Thanks to Trisha Ping and Jennye Garibaldi. Thanks also Dan; Bobby; Dorothy; Trish; Jonah, Mel and Lincoln; Molly, Travis and Sylvie; AJ; Halle and Hugo and Sadie; Adrian, Darcy and Seb; Mike; Nora, David and Dash; and all the crew at UNO. Finally, thanks to my family.

Ray's Thanks

Thanks to my family. Hugs to everyone who showed me around their amazing city: Gimena and Miles, Lindsey and Nick, Barrett, Shemsi, Ilana, Nancy, Henny, Angel and Lexi.

This Book

This 3rd edition of Lonely Planet's *Pocket New Orleans* guidebook was researched and written by Adam Karlin and Ray Bartlett. The previous edition was written by Adam and Amy C Balfour. This guidebook was produced by the following:

Destination Editor Trisha Ping

Senior Product Editors Vicky Smith, Kate Mathews

Product Editor Ronan Abayawickrema

Senior Cartographers Mark Griffiths, Alison Lyall

Cartographer James Leversha

Book Designer Gwen Cotter

Assisting Editors James Bainbridge, Jacqueline Danam, Melanie Dankel, Carly Hall

Cover Researcher Brendan Dempsey-Spencer

Thanks to Imogen Bannister, Celine Baures, Heather Champion, Laura Crawford, David W Greig, Blaze Hadzik, James Hardy, Liz Heynes, Simon Hoskins, Simon Kellogg, Sandie Kestell, Chris Lee Ack, Jean-Pierre Masclef, Liam McGrellis, Dan Moore, Virginia Moreno, Darren O'Connell, Monique Perrin, Martine Power, Kirsten Rawlings, Wibowo Rusli, Dianne Schallmeiner, Ellie Simpson, John Taufa, Angela Tinson, Laura Waters, Carah Whaley, Juan Winata

Our Writers

Adam Karlin

Adam has contributed to dozens of Lonely Planet guidebooks, covering an alphabetical spread that ranges from the Andaman Islands to the Zimbabwe border. As a journalist, he has written on travel, crime, politics, archeology and the Sri Lankan Civil War, among other topics. Adam is based out of New Orleans, which helps explain his love of wetlands, food and good music. Learn more at http://walkon fine.com or follow him on Instagram @adam walkonfine.

Ray Bartlett

Ray has been travel writing for nearly two decades, bringing Japan, Korea, Mexico and many parts of the United States to life in rich detail for top-industry publishers, newspapers and magazines. His acclaimed debut novel, *Sunsets of Tulum*, set in Yucatán, was a *Midwest Book Review* 2016 Fiction pick. Follow him on Facebook, Twitter, Instagram, or contact him via www.kaisora.com, his website. Ray currently divides his time between homes in the USA, Japan and Mexico.

Published by Lonely Planet Global Limited
CRN 554153
3rd edition – Oct 2018
ISBN 978 1 78657 182 3
© Lonely Planet 2018 Photographs © as indicated 2018
10 9 8 7 6 5 4 3 2 1
Printed in Malaysia